OUTLINES OF ISLAM

The Masterpiece Library of ISLAM—2

OUTLINES OF ISLAM

By

T. P. HUGHES

(Edited and Revised Edition)

Introduction By

SYED AMEER ALI

ARYAN BOOKS INTERNATIONAL

NEW DELHI

Outlines of Islam

Published in 2002 By :
ARYAN BOOKS INTERNATIONAL
4378/4B, Pooja Apartments
4B, Ansari Road, Darya Ganj
New Delhi-110002 (India)

ISBN-81-7305-138-0

Printed in India at Print Perfect, New Delhi.

Contents

Preface to the First Edition

There is a general impression amongst European students of Islám, that it is a simple system of Deism unfettered by numerous dogmas and creeds, which are supposed to be such an insuperable hindrance to an acceptance of Christianity. Such was the opinion of the historian, Gibbon, and it is also the view taken by some who seek to weaken the authority of the Christian system by extolling the merit of its great rival creed. But even amongst the advocates of Christianity there is altogether an erroneous impression as to what Muhammadanism really is. Dean Stanley has an admirable chapter on the subject of Islám in his "Eastern Church"; but he tells his readers that, "*the Qurán contains the whole of the religion of Muhammad*"; and Mr. Zincke, in his exceedingly interesting book, "Egypt of the Pharaohs and the Khedive," appears to be under the same impression; for he says, "*the Qurán is an all embracing and sufficient code, regulating everything*." Whereas the true state of the case is, that whilst the Qurán is the highest authority for Muslim doctrine, still, the "faithful," whether Sunní, Shía'h, or Wahhábī, must receive the sayings and practices of their Prophet as of divine obligation; for, in Islám, the teachings of the "Sacred Traditions" must be received side by side with that of the Qurán itself; and the Muslim who would escape the suspicion of heresy must not dare to question the teaching of the learned doctors, whose opinions have been handed down in numerous commentaries and ponderous volumes of divinity.

In publishing these "Outlines of Islam," the author is fully conscious of their imperfections, but he ventures to hope that they will contain information which may be suggestive to Missionaries and others interested in the study of Islám

T. P. H.

Preface to the Second Edition

The favourable reception which has been accorded to the first edition of these outlines of the Muhammadan system has encouraged me to put forth a revised and enlarged edition. I am glad of the opportunity; for, the first edition contained numerous errors, consequent upon my bringing it out during a short and hurried visit to England, in the summer of 1875. Still, notwithstanding its numerous and manifest shortcomings, it has been pronounced by an eminent Arabic scholar, as not only "about the best outlines of Mulsim faith he had seen" ; but having "*the rare merit of being accurate*."

T. P. H.

Introduction

Non-Moslems, unless they have made the teachings of the Arabian Prophet a subject of special study, have generally a very distorted conception of Islâmic morality. They imagine that, with the exception of a few principles, borrowed from Christianity or Judaism, the rest may be summarised in the stern alternative of "the Koran or the sword." Few stop to consider the truth or the meaning of the antithesis; enough that it exists somewhere in the ecclesiastical records of the crusading days. It is impossible to exaggerate the baleful influence of this wholly unjust idea. In this country, English education has deepened the gulf between the two great communities which inhabit the soil of India, by diffusing through the medium of histories written with a bias against Islâm, the notion to which I have referred.

To disabuse people therefore of the impression that Islâm is a religion of force and violence, I give in the following passages a short abstract of the Ethics of Islâm in the words of its great Teacher, of his Disciple, Ali, and of the moralists who have from time to time written on the subject. But before proceeding further I desire to point out that Islâm possesses, in common with all other moral creeds, the everlasting heritage of universal truth. It is to the new life, the new vitality, the vibration it causes to the pulse of humanity that we have to look for the moral force of the creed which wants to take the place of an older faith, and not to what new truths it teaches—for truth cannot be new; it is immutable and eternal like Nature itself.

Such, in my opinion, is the position of Islâm. Its democratic appeal to the conscience of humanity, its assertion of the absolute equality of mankind in the "sight" of the universal Father, its disclaimer of mysteries, its constant affirmation of the intimate communion of the soul of man with its Creator,—appeal more strongly to the ethical faculty of reasonable beings than most other creeds. Legends and stories must grow up as the circle of influence enlarges or time advances,—to suit the tastes and temperaments of the sovereigns as well as the people. No religion has escaped from the effects of this natural desire on the part of man to read the dictates of his particular creed according to his own inclinations.

I trust that the words I wish to quote will help people to see the after all Islâmic morality has as pure aspirations as any other creed; that, instead of inciting people to strife and hostility, it also teaches peace and good-will among mankind in as eloquent terms as any other ethical system.

In order to appreciate the true value of the ethical system of the Arabian Prophet, it must be remembered that in Islâm, the service of man and the good of humanity constitute pre-eminently the service and worship of God Faith without work has no meaning; "this life is but a tillage (*mazraa*) for the next," and therefore we are told repeatedly, "do good that you may reap there." The mere recognition of a creed or formula does not constitute Islâm. It is "a life to be lived in the present." "Dost thou desire to approach thy Lord, act righteously for,—the crooked path never leads to Him." It is pointed out in the language of poetry that man partakes of the nature of the beast as well as of the angel; an he is adjured to leave the nature of the beast, that he may surpass the angel. Striving for the good, the true and the pure is inculcated in the most emphatic terms, "for striving is the ordinance of God, and whatever God has ordained can only be attained by striving."

The Essence of the Islâmic Ethics

The ethical code of Islâm is thus summarised in the fourth Sura of the Koran:—

"Come, I will rehearse what your Lord hath enjoined on you,—that ye assign not to Him a partner, that ye be good to your parents; and that ye slay not your children because of poverty: for them and for you will We provide; and that ye come not near to pollution, outward and inward, and that ye slay not a soul whom God hath forbidden, unless by right.......and draw not nigh to the wealth of the orphan, save so as to better it..... and when ye pronounce judgment then be just, though it be the affair of a kinsman. And God's compact fulfil ye, that is, what He hath ordained to you. Verily, this is my right way; follow it then."

And again, "Blessed are they who believe and humbly offer their thanksgiving to their Lord.....who are constant in their charity, and who guard their chastity, and who observe their trust and convenants.....Verily, God bids you do justice and good, and give to kindred their due; and He forbids you to sin and to do wrong and oppress."

"Who speaketh better than he who inviteth unto God, and worketh good....good and evil shall not be held equal. Turn away evil with that which is better."

Again, speaking of Paradise, it says, "it is prepared for the godly, who give alms in prosperity and adversity; who bridle their anger and forgive men; for God loveth the beneficent."

History has preserved, for the admiration of posterity,

many examples of patience under suffering exhibited by the followers of other creeds. But the practice of the virtues of patient forgiveness is easier in adversity, when we have no power to punish the evil-doer, than in prosperity. It is related of Hussain, the grandson of the Prophet, that a slave having once thrown the contents of a scalding dish over him as he sat at dinner, fell on his knees and repeated the verse of the Koran. "Paradise is for those who bridle their anger." "I am not angry," answered Hussain. The slave proceeded, "and for those who forgive men." "I forgive you." The slave, however, finished the verse adding, "for God loveth the beneficent." "I give you your liberty and four hundred pieces of silver," replied Hussain.

The author of the *Kashshâf* thus sums up the Islâmic teachings: "Seek again him who drives you away; give to him who takes away from you; pardon him who injures you: for God loveth that you should cast into the depth of your souls the roots of his perfections."

The Return of Good for Evil

The return of good for evil is preached on all occasions.—

"Think only of what is good for each, and consider not the wrong that has been done to thee: pardon others readily, and do good unto all. Fair is the dwelling-place of those who have bridled their anger and forgiven their adversaries. Return good for evil."

To the humble denizen of the earth, "with his mouth in the dust," comes the message from Him to lift up the stricken soul.

"By the noonday brightness, and by the night when it darkeneth, thy Lord hath not forsaken thee, neither hath He been displeased. Surely the future shall be better for thee than the past; and in the end He shall be bounteous to thee, and thou shalt be satisfied Did He not find thee an orphan, and give thee a home; erring and guided thee; needy and enriched thee? As to the orphan, then, wrong him not; and chide not away him that asketh of thee, and tell abroad the favours of thy Lord." "Did ye think we had made you for sport, and that ye should not be brought back again to us?"

To the errant sinners, turning with a true penitence to their Creator and crying out to Him,—'O our Lord, punish us not if we forget and fall into sin, blot out our sins, and forgive us,' is conveyed the promise of mercy and forgiveness:—"Come back, come back, whatever thou art, come back; hast thou denied Me or worshipped another for Me, or broken My commandments, come back. This Threshold of Mine is not the threshold of despair. If thou hast forgot thyself, turn with true penitence and come back."

It has been truly said that "the moral idea of the new gospel was set in the common sense of duty and the familiar instances of love."

"Blessed is he who giveth away his substance that he may became pure, and who offereth not favours to any one for the sake of recompense...but only as seeking to approach the Lord Most High."

"They are the blest who, though longing for it themselves, bestowed their food on the poor and the orphan and the captive (saying), 'we feed you for the sake of God: we seek from you neither recompense nor thanks.' "

"Worship God alone; be kind to kindred and servants, orphans and the poor; speak righteously to men, pray, and pay alms."

"Defer humbly to your parents; with humility and tenderness say, 'O Lord, be merciful to them, even as they brought me up when I was helpless.' "

"Abandon the old barbarities, blood-vengeance, and child-murder, and be united as one flesh."

"Do thy alms openly or in secret, for both are well."

"Give of that which hath been given you before the day cometh when there shall be no trafficking, nor friendship, nor interception."

"Wouldst thou be taught the steep path? It is to ransom the captive, to feed the hungry, the kindred, the orphan, and him whose mouth is in the dust. Be of those who enjoin steadfastness and compassion on others."

"Woe to them that make a show of piety, and refuse help to the needy."

"Make not your alms void by reproaches or injury." "Forgiveness and kind speech are better than favours with annoyance." "Abandon usury." "He who spendeth his substance to be seen of men, is like a rock with thin soil over it, whereon the rain falleth and leaveth it hard. But they who expend their substance to please God and establish their souls, are like a garden on a hill, on which the rain falleth and it yieldeth its fruit twofold; and even if the rain doth not fall, yet is there a dew."

"Judge between men with truth and follow not thy passions, lest they cause thee to err from the way of God." "Covet not another's gifts from God." "There is no piety in turning the face east or west, but in believing in God only and doing good." "Make the best of all things; enjoin justice and avoid the foolish; and if Satan stir thee to evil, take refuge in God." "Touch not the goods of the orphan." "Perform your covenant, and walk not proudly on the earth."

"The birth of a daughter brings dark shadows on a man's face........Kill not your children for fear of want: for them and for you will We provide. Verily, the killing them is a great wickedness." "God hath given you wives that ye may put love and tenderness between you."

"Commit not adultery; for it is a foul thing and an evil way."

"Know ye that this world's life is a cheat; the multiplying of riches and children is like the plants that spring up after rain, rejoicing the husbandmen, then turn yellow and wither away. In the next life is severe chastisement, or else pardon from God and his peace." "Abandon wickedness and the very semblance of it. They, verily whose only acquirement is iniquity, shall be rewarded for what they shall have gained." "Those who abstain from vanities and the indulgence of their passions, give alms, offer prayers, and tend well their trusts and their covenants, these shall be the heirs of eternal happiness." "Show kindness to your parents, whether one or both of them attain to old age with thee: and say not to them, 'Fie!' Neither reproach them, but speak to them both with respectful speech and tender affection." "And to him who is of kin render his due, and also to the poor and to the wayfarer, yet waste not wastefully."

"And let not thy hand be tied up to thy neck; nor yet open it with all openness, lest thou set thee down in rebuke in beggary."

"Enjoin my servants to speak in kindly sort." "Turn aside evil with that which is better." "Just balances will We set up for the day of resurrection, neither shall any soul be wronged in ought, though were a work but the weight of a grain of a mustard seed, We would bring it forth to be weighed: and our reckoning will suffice." "Seek pardon of your Lord and beturned unto Him: Verily, my Lord is merciful and loving." "And your Lord saith, 'Call upon Me, I will hearken unto you.' " "Say: 'O my servants who have transgressed to your own injury, despair not of

God's mercy, for all sins doth God forgive. Gracious and merciful is He.' " "The good word riseth up to Him, and the righteous deed will He exalt." "Truly my Lord hath forbidden filthy actions, whether open or secret, and iniquity, and unjust violence."

"Call upon your Lord with lowliness and in secret, for He loveth not transgressors, and commit not disorders on the well-ordered earth after it hath been well ordered; and call on Him with fear and longing desire: verily, the mercy of God is nigh unto the righteous."

"Moreover, We have enjoined on man to show kindness to his parents. With pain his mother beareth him; with pain she bringeth him forth: and he saith, 'O my Lord! Stir me up to be grateful for Thy favours wherewith Thou hast favoured me and my parents, and to do good works which shall please Thee; and prosper me in my offspring: for to Thee am I turned, and am resigned to Thy will.' " "For them is a dwelling of peace with their Lord; and in recompense for their works shall He be their protector." "Lost are they who, in their ignorance, have foolishly slain their children, and have forbidden what God hath given them for food, devising an untruth against God! Now have they erred; and they were not rightly guided."

"The likeness of those who expend their wealth for the cause of God, is that of a grain of corn which produceth seven ears, and in each ear a hundred grains; they who expend their wealth for the cause of God, and never follow what they have laid out with reproaches or harm, shall have their reward with their Lord; nor fear shall come upon them, neither shall they be put to grief;....a kind speech and forgiveness is better than alms followed by injury."

"God will not burden any soul beyond its power. It shall enjoy the good which it hath acquired, and shall bear the evil for the acquirement of which it laboured."......

"O Lord punish us not if we forget or fall into sin, O our Lord! and lay not on us a load like that which Thou hast laid on those who have been before us, O our Lord! and lay not on us that for which we have not strength: but blot out our sins and forgive us and have pity on us."

"The patient and the truthful the lowly and the charitable, and they who seek pardon at each daybreak:" ...... "who give alms, alike in prosperity and in success, and who master their anger, and forgive others! God loveth the doers of good;" [Theirs a goodly home with their Lord]. "O our Lord! forgive us then our sins and hide away from us our evil deeds, and cause us to die with the righteous:" "And their Lord answereth them, 'I will not suffer the work of him among you that worketh, whether of male or female, to be lost, the one of you is the issue of the other.' " "And fear ye God, in whose name ye ask mutual favours,—and reverence your mothers—at their feet is paradise."

"Covet not the gifts by which God hath raised some of you above others."

"Be good to parents, and to kindred, and to orphans, and to the poor, and to a neighbour, whether kinsman or new-comer, and to a fellow-traveller, and to the wayfarer, and to the slaves whom your right hands hold; verily, God loveth not the proud, the vain boaster."

"He who shall mediate between men for a good purpose shall be the gainer by it. But he who shall mediate with an evil mediation shall reap the fruit of it. And God keepeth watch over everything."

"O ye Moslems! stand fast to justice, when ye bear witness before God, though it be against yourselves, or your parents, or your kindred, whether the party be rich or poor. God is nearer than you to both. Therefore follow not passion, lest ye swerve from truth."

Brotherly Love: Mutual Assistance

Brotherly love and mutual assistance are inculcated in emphatic terms:—

"Moslems are brothers in religion; and they must not oppress one another, nor abandon assisting each other, nor hold one another in contempt. The seat of righteousness is the heart; therefore, that heart, which is righteous, does not hold a Moslem in contempt; and it is wicked to hold a Moslem in contempt; and all things of one Moslem are unlawful to another, his blood, property and reputation; he must not act or speak that by which the blood of a Moslem might be spilt, and his property destroyed, and his reputation lost." "The people for Paradise are three; the first, a just king, a doer of good to his people, endowed with virtue; the second, an affectionate man, of a tender heart to relations and others; the third, a virtuous man."

Duties of Mussulmans to Each Other

Again, "The duties of Mussulmans to each other are six." It was asked: "What are they O Prophet?"

He said, "When you meet a Mussulman, *salâm* to him; and when he invites you to dinner, accept it; and when he asks for advice, give it to him; and when he is sick, visit him; and when he dies, follow his bier."

But help to the suffering and the weak is not preached in an exclusive spirit, nor is it confined to Moslems, for it is declared incumbent to assist every oppressed person, whether Moslem or not. "Verily, God will say, at the Day or Resurrection, 'O sons of Adam I was sick, and ye did not visit Me,' and the sons of Adam will say, 'O our Protector how could we visit thee? for thou art Lord of the universe, and art free from sickness.' And God will say, 'O men! Did you not know that such a one of My servants was sick, and ye did not visit him? Did you not know that had you visited that servant, you would have met with favour and pleasure near Me?' And God will say, at the Resurrection, 'O sons of Adam, I asked you for food, and ye gave Me not?' And the sons of Adam will sya, 'O our Lord, how could we give thee food, seeing thou art the Cherisher of the universe and art free from hunger and eating?' And God will say, 'Do not ye know that such a one of My servants asked you for bread, and you did not give it him? Did you know that had you given him victuals, you would have received its reward from Me.' And God will say at the Resurrection, "O sons of Adam! I asked you for water, and ye gave Me not.' They will say, 'O our Cherisher! How could we give thee water, seeing thou art the Cherisher of the universe, and not subject to thirst!' God will say, 'Such an one of My servants asked you for water, and you did not give it him: did you not know that had you given to him, you would have received its reward from Me?' "

Help of the Poor

"That person who asks, in the name of God, protection from harm by you, or from any one else, then give him protection; and that person who asks a thing from you in the name of God, then give it to him, and that person who invites you to eat, approve of and accept his invitation, and that person who does you a good and benefit, then return it, that is, do a good act to him; but if you have nothing to return him, then pray for him, till you know that you have atoned to him and performed your duty to him."

"Do not say, 'if people do good to us, we will do good to them; and if people oppress us, we will oppress them': say, on the contrary, if they oppress you, you will not oppress them."

Kindness to Human Beings

"Whoever is kind to His creatures, God is kind to him; therefore be kind to man on the earth, whether he be good or bad; and being kind to the bad, is to withhold them from badness, so that those who are in heaven may be kind to you."

"Strive always to excel in virtue and truth." "Help each other with generosity and piety. He who helps his fellow brethren and tries to do them good, will receive his reward from the Almighty equal to the reward of those who strive to repress wrong-doing."

"All God's creatures are His family; and he is the most beloved of God who tries to do most good God's creatures."

"The best of men is he from whom good accrues to humanity."

"He who tries to remove the wants of his brother, whether he be successful or not, God will forgive his sins."

"He who helps his brother will himself be helped on the Day of Account."

"The Prophet was asked who was the most favoured of God's creatures. He replied, 'He from whom the greatest good comes to His creatures' And then he was asked what actions are most excellent. He answered, "to gladden the heart of a human being, to feed the hungry, to help the afflicted, to lighten the sorrows of the sorrowful, and to remove the wrongs of the injured.' 'He who helps his fellow creature in the hour of need and he who helps the oppressed, God will help him in the Day of Travail.' "

"Thus saith your Lord, 'whilst living, rely on Me for I am all sufficient; do not be avaricious or covet the goods of your brethren; love for them what you love for yourself; guard yourselves from anger, passion and greed, for these are the worst of actions.' "

"He who is subservient to his passions and desires, and forgets in their pursuits his duty to others, is the worst and weakest of God's creatures." "Be persistent in good actions."

"To gladden the heart of the weary, to remove the suffering of the afflicted has its own reward. In the day of trouble, the memory of the action comes like the rush of a torrent and takes away our burden."

"No man is true in the truest sense of the word, but he who is true in word, in deed and in thought."

"He is true who protects his brother both present and absent."

"Fidelity and truth, purity and gentleness, generosity and sweetness are the best of qualities in man."

A few of the aphorisms of the first Imâm, selected at random from the *Ghurrar-wa'd-Durrar*, will throw light on the teachings of the Mosque in the days of the Republic.

"He who is most dutiful to those to whom he owes duty is the wisest among you."... "He who is the most learned is the best conducted and behaved in his life. He is the most intelligent is the most virtuous"... "No evil is worse than avarice." "To be kind is one of the best of virtues; to tell falsehood one of the worst of vices. He who fulfils his word is one of the noblest of God's creations."

"A bad temper is the worst of afflictions." "To keep free from pollutions is the best of worship. To void evil actions is the best of actions."

"He who sees his own faults is the wisest of men. He who considers himself wiser than others, is the most foolish."

"The worship of God, without gratitude to man, is watering the sand of the desert."

"Fidelity is the beacon which lights the way to heaven."

"Learning is of no value without work; precept of no avail without practice."

"To be forbearing to the faults of your fellow-brethren is an act of charity."

"When you speak, speak the truth; when you attain to power, gently and beneficently with those subordinate to you. When you fall into affliction, be patient; when you have to inflict a punishment, be merciful. When you commit a fault, ask pardon. When you are placed in the seat of justice, be just. When you commit sin, be ashamed. When you see the oppressed, render help."

"Be grateful to those who benefit you. Humility increases your worth. Remembrance of God brings down His mercy."

"He who imparts learning never dies."

"Do not look at the person who speaks, but look at what he speak."

"For the envious, there is no peace. Where there is spite, there can be no true friendship."

"The untruthful knows no modesty."

"No provision [for the next world] is better than piety or doing good actions in this world."

"A man who is the slave of his passions, is the worst of all slaves; and no man has a greater enemy than his own selfishness."

"No action is good unless, the intention is good; nor any word pure unless accompanied by pure action."

"No evil is greater than evil propensities."

"Avarice kills truth."

"Knowledge is the best of blessings."

"Purity of heart is the essence of all virtues."

"Ignorance is the worst of all poverty."

"Kindness and courtesy are better than conferring an obligation."

"To overlook the faults of others is better than almsgiving."

"To forgive when it is in your power to avenge an injury, to love when you are wronged, are the best of virtues."

"Hypocrisy is the destruction of piety; to impose an obligation is destructive of charity; selfishness is destructive of wisdom."

"The good you do alone goes with you into the next world." "Good acts are the steps which take ye to God."

"The peace of the two worlds is a commentary on two words,—love for friends, charity towards enemies."

"On the tablet of my heart I have engraved from the sayings of my father, may his memory be sacred to eternity,—'My child, should you be in the company of one who is fallen, do not be impertinent and do not view him with the eyes of contempt; if, in this world, you cannot make a heart glad, yet act not so as to make the humblest soul sorrowful,' "

"O thou who hast experienced happiness and trouble from good and bad events, and who art in consequence full of thanks, and sometimes of complaints ! Do not take high ground, that thy efforts be not vain; be rather like grass, that stands in the way of the wind, or like a bundle of grass, which others carry off on their shoulders."

Tenderness for Children and Respect Forage

Tenderness and affection for children and respect for age are emphatically inculcated. "He is not of us, who is not affectionate to his little ones, and does not respect the reputation of the old; and he is not of us, who does not order that which is lawful, and prohibit that which is unlawful."

"Every young person who honours the old, on account of their age, may God appoint those, in his years, to honour him." "Whoever puts his hand upon the head of an orphan, from kindness, shall have the blessings of God, for every hair his hand shall have covered; and whoever does good to a boy or girl, being orphans, he and I shall be near each other in paradise." "Whoever gives an orphan a dwelling, meat and drink, God will bestow him a place in paradise and forgive his sins."

"He who is not affectionate to God's creation, and to his own children, God will not be affectionate to him."

Sympathy with the Suffering

Sympathy with suffering and tenderness to the woe-stricken and lonely are taught as the highest duties.

"God is merciful to those who are merciful to His creatures."

"Pardon the sins of others that you may be pardoned. If you seek for mercy, be pitiful to the sufferings of mankind."

"He who is kind to an orphan will receive God's blessing on the Day of Account."

"Verily a man's children are God's gifts."

"He who is merciful to others will himself receive mercy; he who has pity for other's wrongs will himself be pitied by the Lord of the Universe."

"He who does not forgive, will not be forgiven himself."

" 'O my servants,' says the Almighty, 'if you seek My mercy, be merciful to My creatures.' "

"They will enter the abode of bliss who have a true, pure and merciful heart"

"The best of almsgiving is that which springs from the heart, and is uttered by the lips to soften the wounds of the injured."

"Modesty and chastity are parts of the Faith."

"He who is modest and chaste, nobody should find fault with him."

"True modesty is the source of all virtues."

"Humility and courtesy are acts of piety."

"Forgive others, incite all to do good and abstain from wickedness."

"Avoid evil-doers and vain speakers and those who speak falsely."

"God loves those who suppress their anger when angry, and forgive people, and do what is right, and act piously and purely."

"The patient, the forbearing and those who forgive the faults of others, having the power to punish, will receive the reward from their Lord."

"Thus saith your Lord, 'Verily those who are patient in adversity and forgive wrongs are the doers of excellence.' "

"The faithful are those who perform their trust and fail not in their word and keep their pledge."

Prophet

"He is not of me but a rebel at heart who, when he speaks, speaks falsely; who, when he promises, breaks his promises; and who, when trust is reposed in him, fails in his trust."

Meanness and slander, hypocrisy and untruthfulness are denounced.

"I heard the Prophet say," says one of the traditionists, " 'it is better to sit alone than in company with the bad; and it is better to sit with the good than alone; and it is better to speak words to a seeker of knowledge than to remain silent; and silence is better than bad words. I advise you to be righteous to God, because it will adorn you in every work, withhold yourself from seeing the vices of mankind, and from giving them utterance.' "

Self-abnegation and patience are laid down as supreme duties:—

"Love is the abnegation of self for another; Divine love is complete self-absorption in the service of God's creatures for His pleasure."

"Patience is the recognition of God's will in the wrongs of life. Thankfulness is the overflowing of the heart with the fullness of His mercy. Acquiescence (*raza*) is the acceptance with thankfulness of God's will."

"He that is patient and thankful, loving and gentle to God's creatures, and returns good for evil, and subdues his passion, and forgets his own self for others—will receive a great reward in that he will approach his Lord."

The Persian moralist Saadi speaks of the virtue of patience in these terms:—

"A great river is not made turbid by a stone; the religious man who takes to heart an injury is as yet but shallow water. If any misfortune befalleth you, bear with it, that, by forgiving, others, you may yourself obtain pardon. O my brother ! seeing that we are at last to return to earth, let us humble ourselves in ashes before we are changed into dust."

Fidelity and truth are most impressively inculcate:—

"When you speak, speak the truth; perform when you promise; discharge your trust; commit not fornication; be chaste; have no impure desires; withhold your hands from striking, and from taking that which is unlawful and bad. The best of God's servants are those who when seen, remind of God; and the worst of God's servants are those who carry tales about, to do mischief and separate friends, and seek for the defects of the good."

Family love and affection are recommended as highly meritorious:—

"Verily there are some of God's servants, who are neither Prophets nor Martyrs, who will emulate Prophets and Martyrs on the day of Resurrection on account of their high eminence near God. They are a family loving each other, for God's favour, befriending each other to please God and to obtain His love."

The attainment of God's love is inculcated in the following words which the Almighty addresses to mankind:—

"Whoever seeks to approach Me by that which I have given as My divine commands, is most loved by Me, and My servant is always seeking to approach Me by holiness; so that I love him: therefore, when I hold him as a friend, I am his hearing by which he hears, and I am his sight by which he sees, and I am his hand by which he holds, and I am his feet by which he walks; if this servant supplicates Me, verily I give unto him; and, if he seeks protection with Me from harm and ills, I give him protection."

Humanity to Living Creatures

It is laid down repeatedly that not only does God reward good done to human beings, but to all living creatures.

"A woman who had sinned was passing by a dog which was holding out its tongue from thirst, and was near to dying. The woman drew off her boot and tied it to the end of her garment, and drew water for the dog, and gave it to drink; the Lord forgave her sin." The Prophet was asked, "Verily are there rewards for our doing good to quadrupeds, and giving them water to drink?" He said, "there are rewards for benefiting every living creature."

A man once came to him with a bundle and said: "O Prophet, I passed through a wood and heard the voices of the young of birds, and I took them up and put them into my carpet, and their mother came fluttering round my head." And the Prophet said: "put them down;" and when he had put them down, the mother joined the young. And the Prophet said: "Do you wonder at the affection of the mother towards her young ? I swear by Him who has sent me, verily, God is more loving to His servants than the mother to these young birds. Return them to the place from which ye took them, and let their mother be with them." "Fear God with regard to animals," used he to say; "ride them when they are fit to be ridden, and get off when they are tired. Verily, there are rewards for our doing good to dumb animals, and giving them water to drink."

Charity

The Prophet's definition of charity embraced the wide circle of kindness: "Every good act," he would say, "is charity. Your smiling in your brother's face is charity; an exhortation addressed to your fellow-men to do virtuous deeds is equal to almsgiving. Putting a wanderer in the right path is charity; assisting the blind is charity; removing stones and thorns and other obstructions from the road is charity; giving water to the thirsty is charity."

"A man's true wealth hereafter is the good he does in this world to his fellow-men. When he dies, people will ask, What property has he left behind him? But the angels who examine him in the grave, will ask, What good deeds hast thou sent before thee?"

He would often tell his disciples, “Do not think any good act done to you contemptible; and I advise you, that you speak to your brother with an open countenance, because that is of the number of good acts and kindnesses. And if a man abuse you, and lay open a vice which he knows in you, then do not disclose one which you know in him, so that there may be no fault but on him.”

Charity to Kindred

Charity to one’s kindred is placed in the first rank.

“Giving alms to the poor has the reward of one benefaction, but that given to kindred has two rewards; one, the reward of charity, the other the reward for relationship.”

The following anecdote will show the value attached to family obligations and the merit of benefactions to one’s children:—A man came to the Prophet and said, “I have got one dinâr.” He said, “Expend it upon yourself.” The man said, “I have got another dinâr.” The Prophet said, “Expend that upon your children.” The man said, “I have got another dinâr.” He said, “Expend that upon your wife and your parents and poor relations.” He said, “I have got one other dinâr.” The Prophet said, “Expend that upon your servants.” The man said, “I have got another dinâr.” “You know best the person most worthy of it; and whoever you know to be so, give it to him.”

“Whatever we give” says the author of the *Akhlâk-i-Jelâli*, “should be given in the fulness of zeal and good-will, and never be the least regretted either in word or thought. For it would be the height of folly, when God, from the treasure-house of his bounty, has given a fortune to one of his servants, subject to the expenditure in a particular manner of an insignificant fraction, for him to consider the condition as burdensome to discharge. We should spend it simply to please God, and not mix up the act with any meaner motive, lest thereby it be rendered null and void.

We should bestow what we give on such as make a secret of their poverty; we should give in secret: or the ostentation of repute is folly. We find it among the *ahâdis*:—(the traditions of the Prohet) 'Charity that is concealed appeaseth the wrath of God.' And, again, 'The best of alms is that which the light hand giveth and the left knows not of.' From the Prophet we also have it, that when the just and holy God created the earth, it trembled and could not rest; whereupon He created the mountains to keep it still. At this the angels marvelled and inquired whether any created thing were stronger than a mountain? He told them, yes, fire. Again, they asked whether any thing were stronger than fire? He told them, yes, water. Any thing stronger than water? Yes, wind. Any thing stronger than wind? Yes, alms concealed, which the son of Adam giveth, so that the right hand gives, and the left knows it not. Of this the influence is greatest of any; for it averteth the scourge that is ready to fall."

In the battle of life men and women have always felt the need of help from a Power above and beyond themselves whose love is boundless and universal. Is not the human soul better and purer for seeking the help of its Maker in the trials of life? The following prayer shows the value attached in Islâm to the outpouring of the human soul to the Giver of all good:—

"We have reached the night, and so have all other inhabitants of God's empire. Praised be God, one to whom there is no partner; for Him is dominion and praise, and He is powerful over all things. O God ! I supplicate Thee for the good of this night, and for every good that is in it; and I seek protection with Thee, from the evils of this night, and from every evil that may be in it. O Lord ! Verily, I seek protection with Thee from sickness, from age and pride; and from the contentions and calamities of the world and from the punishment of the grave. O Lord ! I have resigned my soul to Thy commands and turned to Thee. I have made over my work to Thee, and relied on Thee, and sought protection in Thee, to show my love to Thee; and for fearing Thee, there is no asylum or redemption from Thy resentment but in Thee."

"O Lord ! Pardon my faults, and the works which I may have done through ignorance; and forgive my lavishing away, and pardon my sins, which Thou knowest better than me. O Lord ! Pardon me my inconsiderate speaking, and blundering; and forgive my wicked labours and intentions and all these are my characteristics. O Lord! Pardon me the faults which I have done before, and shall do after, and those which I have discovered and concealed; and those which Thou knowest better than me. Thou art the first and the last, and powerful over everything."

"O Lord ! Make me a thanksgiver to Thee, and a repeater of Thy name, and a fearer of thee, and a great obeyor of Thee, and a great humbler of myself before Thee, and complainer and repenter to Thee. O Lord ! Accept my repentance and wash away my sins and approve my supplications; and strengthen my proofs, and make my tongue true; and show my heart the straight road; and remove away the wicked inclinations of my heart."

A learned critic has called the virtues of Islâm, "stoical" The expression was used in an invidious sense, but if patience, forbearance, charity, truth, purity and magnanimity were the distinguishing characteristics of Stoics, I am prepared to admit that the ethical duties of Islâm are stoical. In the *Akhlâk*, magnanimity is defined thus:—

"That the soul take no note of honour or disrepute, pay no regard to affluence or adversity, but remain entirely unaffected by praise or censure, by wealth or want; from the mutations of human affairs admitting neither alteration nor transition, nor impression, nor influence: a spiritual eminence whose heights are only attainable to the most advanced on the paths of research; whose submits are not to be contemplated, but by the choicest of the accomplished."

"He is a man," says the Allâmah Abul Fazl, "of high understanding and noble aspirations, who, without the help of others, recognises a ray of the divine power in the smallest things of the world; who shapes his inward and outward character accordingly, and shows due respect to himself and to others. True greatness, in spiritual and in worldly matters, does not shrink from the *minutiæ* of business, but regards their performance as an act of divine worship."

"Every man of sense and understanding knows that the best way of worshipping God is in allaying the distress of the times, and in improving the condition of man."

"Have the religions of the worldly tendencies of mankind no common ground? Is there not everywhere the same enrapturing beauty which beams forth from so many thousand hidden places? Broad indeed is the carpet which God has spread, and beautiful the colours which he has given it."

Humility

At the same time men are taught to be humble.

"O men! be humble and lowly. He who guards his tongue from detraction, God will conceal his vices; and he who suppresses his anger, God will withhold His punishments from him; and he who asks pardon of God, God will accept his supplication."

"Whatever jewels thou wearest on thy brow, only humility can give them their lustre. To that talisman paradise opens its gate, and to it opens the heart of man. Dear to all hearts is he whom lowliness exalts; his bending is the graceful droop of the branch laden with fruit."

Dignity of Labour

The dignity of labour preached in emphatic terms.

"There is a tradition from the Prophet," says Tirmizi, "that a man of the Ansâr came to him begging for some help; and the Prophet said, 'Have you nothing at home?' He said, 'Yes, there is a large carpet, with one part of which I cover myself, and spread the other, and there is a wooden cup out of which I drink water.' The Prophet said, 'Bring me the carpet and the cup.' And the man brought them, and the Prophet took them in his hands and said, 'Who will buy them?' A man said, 'I will take them at one dirhem.' 'He said, 'Who will give more?' This be repeated twice or thrice. Another man said, 'I will take them for two dirhems.' Then the Prophet gave the carpet and cup to that man, and took the two dirhems, which he gave to the Ansâr and said, 'Buy food with one of these dirhems and give it to your family, that they make it their sustenance for a few days; and buy a hatchet with the other dirhem and bring it to me.' And the man brought it; and the Prophet put a handle to it with his own hands, and then said, 'Go, cut wood and sell it; and let me not see you for fifteen days.' Then the man went cutting wood and selling it: and he came to the Prophet, when verily, he had got ten dirhems; and he bought a garment with part of them, and food with part. Them the Prophet said, "This cutting and selling of wood, and making your livelihood by it, is better for these than begging."

Idleness Reprehended

Idleness is reprehended "God is gracious to him who ears his living by his own labour and not by begging."

"He who is able and fit and does not work for himself or for others, God is not gracious to him."

"He who works for his own living and does not beg, when he can earn, is one of God's favoured creatures."

"He who neither works for himself nor for others, will not receive the reward of God."

"Pray to God morning and evening and employ the day in your avocations."

The Charge of obscurantism can hardly be laid against Islâm, when it is considered how eloquently the Founder recommended the acquisition of knowledge to his followers:—

Knowledge

"Acquire knowledge," he used to say, "because he who acquires it in the way of the Lord performs an act of piety; who speaks of it, praises the Lord; who seeks it, adores God; who dispenses instruction in it, bestows alms; and who imparts it to its fitting objects, performs an act of devotion to God. Knowledge enables its possessor to distinguish what is forbidden from what is not; it lights the way to Heaven; it is our friend in the desert, our society in solitude, our companion when bereft of friends; it guides us to happiness, it sustains us in misery; it is our ornament in the company of friends; it serves as an armour against our enemies. With knowledge, the servant of God rises to the heights of goodness and to a noble position, associates with sovereigns in this world, and attains to the perfection of happiness in the next."

"The ink of the scholar is more holy than the blood of the martyr."

"He who leaves his home in search of knowledge, walks in the path of God."

"He who travels in search of knowledge, to him God shows the way to paradise."

"One hour's meditation on the work of the Creator [in a devout spirit] is better than seventy years' prayer."

"To listen to the instruction of science and learning for one hour is more meritorious than attending the funerals of a thousand martyrs,— more meritorious than standing up in prayer for a thousand nights."

"To the student who goes forth in quest of knowledge, God will allot a high place in the mansions of bliss; every step he takes is blessed, and every lesson he receives has its retard. The seeker of knowledge will be greeted in heaven with a welcome from the angels. To listen to the words of the learned, and to instil into the heart the lessons of science, is better than religious exercises. . . .better than emancipating a hundred slaves. Him, who favours learning and the learned, God will favour in the next world."

"He who honours the learned, honours me."

"Eminence in science is the highest of honours. He dies not who gives life to learning. The greatest ornament of a man is erudition."

"The world is darkness; knowledge is light; but knowledge without truth is a mere shadow."

Man's responsibility was laid down in explicit terms.

"Whosoever gets to himself a sin, gets it solely at his own responsibility."

"And let alone those who make a sport and mockery of their religion, and whom this present world has deluded, and thereby bring to remembrance that the soul perishes of what it has got to itself, and when they commit a deed of shame they say: 'We have found that our fathers did so, and God obliges us to do it:' say thou: 'Surely, God requireth not shameful doing;... they did injustice to themselves; yonder will every soul experience that which it hath bargained for;'. . . so then, whosoever is directed, it is solely a matter pertaining to himself; and whosoever goes astray, he himself bears the whole responsibility of his wanderings."

In the purity of its aspirations can anything be more beautiful than the following:—

"The servants of the Merciful are they that walk upon the earth softly, and when the ignorant speak unto them, they reply 'Peace !' They that spend the light worshipping their Lord prostrate and standing and resting, those that, when they spend are neither profuse nor niggardly, but take a middle course. . .those that invoke not with God any other God and slay not a soul that God hath forbidden otherwise than by right, and commit not fornication . . they who bear not witness to that which is false; and when they pass by vain sport, they pass it by with dignity, who say, 'Oh, our Lord, grant us of our wives and children such as shall be a comfort unto us, and make us examples unto the pious,'—these shall be the rewarded, for that they persevered; and they shall be accosted in paradise with welcome and salutation:—For ever therein,—a fair abode and resting-place !"

Syed Ameer Ali

1
Muhammad

The earliest biographers of the Arabian Prophet, whose works are extant in Arabic, are Ibn-Isháq (A.H. 151), Ibn-Hishám (A.H. 218), Wáqidi (A.H. 207), and Tabari (A.H. 310). Ismail Abulfida, Prince of Hamah, in Syria (A.H. 733), compiled a Life of Muhammad in Arabic, which was translated by John Gagnier, Professor of Arabic at Oxford (A.D. 1723), and into English by the Rev. W. Murray, Episcopal clergyman at Duffus, in Scotland.[1] Dr. Sprenger of Calcutta commenced a Life of Muhammad in English, and printed the first part of it at Allahabad (A.D. 1851); but it was never completed. The learned author afterwards published his work in German in 1869.[2] The only Life of Muhammad in English, which has any pretension to original research, is that by Sir William Muir of the Bengal Civil Service.[3]

Muhammad (lit. *the praised one*), son of Abdul Muttalib, by his wife Amina, was born at Mecca at, August 29th, A.D. 570. He assumed the prophetic office at the age of forty, fled from Mecca at the age of fifty-four, and died at Medinah, June 9th, A.D. 632, aged sixty-two

The *Hijrat*, or Hegira (the flight from Mecca), which is the Muhammadan era, dates from July 16th, A.D. 622.

In forming an estimate of Muhammad's prophetical pretensions, it must be remembered that he did not claim to be the founder of a new religion, but merely of a new covenant. He is the last and greatest of all God's prophets. He is sent to convert the world to the one true religion We follow the prophet in his self-asserted mission from the cave of Hira to the closing scene, when he dies in the midst of the lamentations of his harem, and the contentions of his friends—the visions of Gabriel, the period of mental depression, the contemplated suicide, the assumption of the prophetic office, his struggles with Meccan unbelief, his flight to Medina, his triumphant entry into Mecca—and we wonder at the genius of the hero.

We are not insensible to the beauties of the Qurán as a literary production, and we admire its conceptions of the Divine nature, its deep and fervent trust in the power of God, its frequent deep moral earnestness, and its sententious wisdom.

References

1. Mr. Murray's translation was published at Elgin (without date). It is exceedingly scarce, the British Museum not possessing a copy.
2. Das Leben und die Lehre des Mohammad. A. Sprenger. 6 vols. 8vo. Berlin, 1869.
3. Life of Mahomet. 4 vols. 8vo. London, 1858–61. New Edition. 1 vol. 8vo. London, 1877.

2
Islam

Islam is the name given to the Muhammadan religion by its founder. Abdul Haqq (the commentator on the Mishkát) says it implies "submission to the divine will."

In the Dictionary of the Qurán entitled Moghrab, *Islám* is explained as "entering into peace (*salm*) with another," alluding to the fact that he who embraces Islám in a Muhammadan state becomes free from all those penalities and disabilities which belong to one who does not embrace the faith.

In the Qurán the word is used for doing homage to God. Islám is said to be the religion of all the prophets from the time of Abraham, as will appear from the following verses (Surat-ul-Imrán, ver. 78, 79) : "We believe in God and in what hath been sent down to Abraham, and Ishmael, and Isaac, and Jacob, and the Tribes, and in what was given to Moses, and Jesus and the Prophets from their Lord. We make no difference between them, and to him are we resigned (*i.e Muslims*). Whose desireth any other religion than *Islám*, that religion shall never be accepted of him, and in the next world he shall be lost."

There are three words used by Muhammadan writers for religion, namely, *Dín, Millat*, and *Mazhab*; and in the Kitáb-ut-Táriífát the difference implied in these words is said to be as follows : *Dín* as it stands in its relation to

God, *e.g. Dín-Ullah*, the religion of God; *Millat,* as it stands in relation to a prophet or lawgiver, e.g. *Millat-i-Ibrahím*, the religion of Abraham; and *Mazhab* as it stands in relation to the divines of Islám, *e.g. Mazhab-i-Hanafí*, the religion of Hanífa. The expression *Dín*, however, is of general application.

Those who profess of religion of Islám are called Musalmáns, Muslims, or Momins.

Ahl-i-Kitáb "the people of the Book," is used for Muhammadans, Jews and Christians.

3
Rule of Faith

The Muhammadan rule of faith is based upon what are called the four foundations of orthodoxy, namely, the *Qurán*, or, as it is called *Kalám Ullah*, the Word of God; the *Hadis* (pl. *Ahádís*), or the traditions of the saying and practice of Muhammad; *Ijmá'*, or the consent of the Mujtahidín, or learned doctors; and *Qiás*, or the analogical reasoning of the learned.

In studying the Muhammadan religious system it must be well understood that Islám is not simply the religion of the Qurán, but that all Muhammadans, whether Sunni, Shía'h, or Wahhábi, receive the Traditions as an authority in matters of faith and practice. The *Sunni* Muhammadans arrogate to themselves the title of traditionists; but the Shía'hs also receive the Hadís as binding upon them, although they do not acknowledge the same collection of traditions as those received by their opponents. The Wahhábis receive the "six correct books of the Sunnis"

The *example* of Muhammad is just as binding upon the Muslim, as that of Him who said, "Learn of me" is upon the Christian, and very many were the injunctions which the "Prophet" gave as to the transmission of his sayings and practice, and very elaborate is the *canon* whereby Muslims arrive at what they believe to be the example of their Prophet. If, therefore, the grand and elaborate system of morals as expressed in the law of Islám has failed to raise the standard of morality amongst the nations of the earth which have embraced its creed, it is not unreasonable to conclude that its failure rests in the absence of a living example of truth.

4
The Qurán[1]

The word *Qurán* is derived from the Arabic *Qara*, which occurs at the commencement of Súra xcv., which is said to have been the first chapter revealed to Muhammad; and has the same meaning as the Hebrew *kara*, "to read," or "to recite," which is frequently used in Jeremiah xxxvi., as well as in other places in the Old Testament. It is, therefore, equivalent to the Hebrew *mikra,* rendered in Nehemiah viii. 18. "the reading." It is the title given to the Muhammadan Scriptures which are usually appealed to and quoted from as the "*Qurán Majid,*" or the "Glorious Qurán"; the "*Quran Sharíf,*" or the "Noble Qurán"; and is also called the "*Fúrqán,*" or "Distinguisher," "*Kalám Ullah,*" or the "Word of God." and "*Al kitáb*," or "the Book."[2]

Muhammadans believe the Qurán to be the inspired Word of God sent down to the lowest heaven complete,[3] and then revealed from time to time to the Prophet by the Angel Gabriel.

There is, however, only one[4] distinct assertion in the Qurán to Gabriel having been the medium of inspiration, namely, Súra-i-Baqr (ii.), 91; and this occurs in a Medina Súra, revealed about seven years after the Prophet's rule had been established. In the Súra-i-Shura (xxvi.), 192, the Qurán is said to have been given by the "*Rúh ul A'mín,*" or Faithful Spirit; and in the Súra-i-Najm (liii.), 5,

Muhammad claims to have been taught by the *"Shadíd-ul-Quá,"* or One terrible in power; and in the Traditions the agent of inspiration is generally spoken of as "an angel" (*malak*).[5] It is, therefore, not quite certain through what agency Muhammad believed himself to be inspired of God.

According to Anyeshah, one of the Prophet's wives, the revelation was first communicated in dreams. Ayeshah relates[6] : — "The first revelations which the Prophet received were in true dreams; and he never dreamt but it came to pass as regularly as the dawn of day. After this the Prophet was fond of retirement, and used to seclude himself in a cave in mount Híráa and worship there day and night. He would, whenever he wished, return to his family at Mecca, and then go back again, taking with him the necessaries of life. Thus, he continued to return to Khadíjah from time to time, until one day the revelation came down to him, and the angel (*malak*)[7] came to him and said, 'Read' (*igaráa*); but the Prophet said, 'I am not a reader.' And the Prophet related, that he (*i.e.* the angel) took hold of me and squeezed me as much as I could bear, and he then let me go and said again, 'Read!' And I said, 'I am not a reader.' Then he took hold to me a second time, and squeezed me as much as I could bear, and then let me go, and said 'Read!' And I said, 'I am not a reader.' Then he took hold of me a third time and squeezed me as much as I could bear, and said :—

" 'Read! in the name of thy Lord who created;
Created man from a clot of blood in the womb.

" 'Read! for thy Lord is the most beneficent,
He hath taught men the use of the pen;
He hath taught man that which he knoweth not.'[8]

"Then the Prophet repeated the words himself, and with his heart trembling he returned (*i.e.,* from Híráa to

Mecca) to Khadíjah, and said, 'Wrap me up, wrap me up.' And they wrapped him up in a garment till his fear was dispelled, and he told Khadíjah what had passed, and he said : 'Verily, I was afraid I should have died.' Then Khadíjah said, 'No, it will not be so. I swear by God, He will never make you melancholy or sad. For verily you are kind to your relatives, you speak the truth, you are faithful in trust, you bear the afflictions of the people, you spend in good works what you gain in trade, you are hospitable, and you assist your fellow men.' After this, Khadíjah took the Prophet to Waraqa, who was the son of her uncle, and she said to him, 'O son of my uncle! hear what your brother's son says.' Then Waraqa said to the Prophet, 'O son of my brother! what do you see?' Then the Prophet told Waraqa what he saw, and Waraqa said, 'That is the *Námús*[9] which God sent to Moses.' Ayeshah also relates that Haris-ibn-Hishám asked the Prophet, 'How did the revelation come to you?' and the Prophet said, 'Sometimes like the noise of a bell, and sometimes the angle would come and converse with me in the shape of a man.' "

According to A'yeshah's statement, the Súra-i-Alaq (xcvi.) was the first portion of the Qurán revealed; but it is more probable that the poetical Súras, in which there is no express declaration of the prophetic office, or of a divine commission, were composed at an earlier period. Internal evidence would assign the earliest date to the Súras Zilzál (xcix.), Asar (ciii.), A'diyát (c.), and Fátiha (i.), which are rather the utterances of a searcher after truth than of an Apostle of God.

The whole book was not arranged until after Muhammad's death, but it is believed that the Prophet himself divided the Suras and gave most of them their present titles, which are chosen from some word which occurs in the chapter.[10] The following is the account of the collection and arrangement of the Qurán, as it stands at present, as given in traditions recorded by Bokhárí:—

"Zaid-ibn-Sábit, relates[11]:— 'Abú-Bakr sent a person to me, and called me to him, at the time of the battle with the people of Zemámah; and I went to him, and Omar was with him; and Abú-Bakr said to me, "Omar came to me and said, 'Verily, a great many of the readers of the Qurán were slain on the day of the battle with the people of Zemámah; and really I am afraid that if the slaughter should be great, much will be lost from the Qurán, because every person remembers something of it; and, verily, I see it advisable for you to order the Qurán to be collected into one book.' I said to Omar, 'How can I do a thing which the 'Prophet has not done?' He said, 'I swear by God, this collecting of the Qurán is a good thing.' And Omar used to be constantly returning to me and saying: 'You must collect the Qurán,' till at length God opened my breast so to do, and I saw what Omar had been advising.' And Zaid-ibn-Sábit says that, 'Abú-Bakr said to me, "You are a young and sensible man, and I do not suspect you of forgetfulness, negligence, or perfidy; and, verily, you used to write for the Prophet his instructions from above; then look for the Qurán in every place and collect it." I said, "I swear by God, that if people had ordered me to carry a mountain about from one place to another, it would not be heavier upon me than the order which Abú-Bakr has given for collecting the Qurán." I said to Abú-Bakr, "How do you do a thing which the Prophet of God did not?" He said, "By God, this collecting of the Qurán is a good act." And he used perpetually to return to me, until God put it into my heart to do the thing which the heart of Omar had been set upon. Then I sought for the Qurán, and collected it from the leaves of the date, and white stones, and the breasts of people that remembered it, till I found the last part of the chapter entitled *Tauba* (Repentance), with Abú-Khuzaimah Ansárí, and with no other person. These leaves were in the possession of Abú-Bakr, until God caused him to die; after which Omar had them in his life-time; after that, they remained with his daughter, Hafsah; after that, Osmán compiled them into one book.'

"Anas-ibn-Málik relates:— 'Huzaifah came to Osmán, and he had fought with the people of Syria in the conquest of Armenia; and had fought in Azurbaiján, with the people of Irák, and he was shocked at the different ways of people reading the Qurán. And Huzaifah said to Osmán, "O Osmán, assist this people, before they differ in the Book of God, just as the Jews and Christians differ in their books." Then Osmán sent a person to Hafsah, ordering her to send those portions which she had, and saying, "I shall have a number of copies of them taken, and will then return them to you." And Hafsah sent the portions of Osmán, and Osmán ordered Zaid-ibn-Sábit, Ansarı, and Abdullah-bin-Zn-bair, and Said-ibn-Alnas, and Abdulláh-ibn-ul-Háris-bin-Hishám; and these were all of the Quraish tribe, except Zaid-ibn-Sábit and Ósmán. And he said to the three Quraishites, "When you and Zaid-ibn-Sábit differ about any part of the dialect of the Quran, then do ye write it in the Quraish dialect, because it came not down in the language of any tribe but theirs." Then they did as Osmán had ordered; and when a number of copies had been taken, Osmán returned the leaves to Hafsah. And Osmán sent a copy to every quarter of the countries of Islám, and ordered all other leaves to be burnt, and Ibn-Shaháb said, "Kharíjah, son of Zaid-ibn-Sábit, informed me, saying, 'I could not find one verse when I was writing the Qurán, which, verily, I heard from the Prophet; then I looked for it, and found it with Khuzaimah Ansari, and entered it into the Súra-i-Ahzáb.' "

This recension of the Qurán produced by Khalífa Osmán has been handed down to us unaltered; and, as Sir William Muir remarks, "There is probably no other book in the world which has remained twelve centuries with so pure a text."[12]

That various readings (such as Christians understand by the term) did exist when Osmán produced the first uniform edition is more than probable, and the Shi'ahs have always charged the Ansárs[13] with "having mutilated and changed and made the Qurán what they pleased;" a charge, however, which they do not attempt to prove, beyond the mere assertion that certain passages were omitted which favoured the claims of Alí to be the first Khalif.

The various readings (*Qira'at*) in the Qurán are not such as are usually understood by the term in English authors, but different *dialects* of the Arabic language. Ibn Abbas says the Prophet said, "Gabriel taught me to read the Qurán in one dialect, and when I recited it he taught me to recite it in another dialect, and so on until the number of dialects increased to seven."[14]

Muhammad seems to have adopted this expedient to satisfy the desire of the leading tribes to have a Qurán in their own dialect; for Abdul Haqq[15] says, "The Qurán was first revealed in the dialect of the Quraish, which was the Prophet's native tongue; but when the Prophet saw that the people of other tribes recited it with difficulty then he obtained permission from God to extend its currency by allowing it to be recited in all the chief dialects of Arabia, which were seven:— Quaraish, Taí, Hawázin, Ahl-i-Yaman, Saqíf, Huzail, and Baní-Tamín. Everyone of these tribes accordingly read the Qurán in its own dialect, till the time of Osmán, when these differences of reading were prohibited."

These seven dialects are called *Saba'ta-Ahrúf*, and the science of reading the Qurán in the correct dialect is called *'Ilm-i-Tajwíd*.

The chronological arrangement of the chapters of the Qurán is most important. In the present Urdú edition, as well as in all Arabic editions, the Súrás are placed as they must have been arranged by Zaid-ibn-i-Sábit, who put them together regardless of all chronological sequence. If, therefore, we arrange them according to the order which is given in Syruty's Itqán,[16] we shall not fail to mark the gradual development of Muhammad's mind from that of a mere moral teacher and reformer, to that of a prophet and warrior chief. The contrast between the earlier, middle, and later Súrás is very striking. He who at Mecca is the admonisher and persuader, at Medína is the legislator and the warrior, who dictates obedience, and uses other weapons than the pen of the poet and the scribe. When business pressed, as at Medına, poetry makes way for prose; and although touches of the poetical element occasionally break forth, and he has to defend himself up to a very late period against the charge of being merely a poet, yet this is rarely the case in the Medína Súrás, in which we so frequently meet with injunctions to obey God and the Prophet.[17]

To fully realize the gradual growth of Muhammad's religious system in his own mind, it is absolutely necessary to read the Qurán through, not in the order in which it now stands, but that in which Muslim divines admit that it was revealed. At the same time it must be remembered that all Muhammadan doctors allow that in most of the Súrás there are verses which belong to a different date from that of other portions of the chapter; for example, in the Síra-i-'Alaq the first five verses belong to a much earlier date than the others; and in Síra-i-Baqr, verse 234 is acknowledged by all commentators to have been revealed after verse 240, which it abrogates.

The Qurán is divided into :—

1. *Harf* (pl. *Hurúf*), Letters; of which there are said to be 323,671.
2. *Kalimah* (pl. *Kalimát*), Words; of which there are 77,934.
3. *A'yat* (pl. *A'yát*), Verses. A'yát is a word which signifies "signs," and it was used by Muhammad for short sections or verses of his supposed revelation. There are said to be 6,616 verses in the whole book; but the division of verses differs in different editions of the Arabic Qurán. The number of verses in the Arabic Quráns are recorded after the title of the Súra, and the verses distinguished in the text by a small cypher of circle.[19]
4. *Súra* (pl. *Suwar*), Chapters. A word which signifies a row or series, but which is now used exclusively for the chapters of the Qurán, which are one hundred and fourteen in number. These chapters are called after some word which occurs in the text, and if the Traditions are to be trusted, they were so named by Muhammad himself, although the verses of their respective Súrás were undoubtedly arranged after his death, and sometimes with little regard to their sequence. Musalmán doctors admit that the Khalif Osmán arranged the chapters in the order in which they now stand in the Qurán.
5. *Ruku'* (pl. *Rúkúát*), Prostrations. These are of two kinds, the *Rukú'* of a Súra and the *Rukú*, of

a Sípára, and are distinguished in the Arabic Qurán by the letter *'ain* on the margin. Muhammadans generally quote by the Rukú and not by the verse.

6. *Ruba'*, The quarter of a Sípára.
7. *Nisf*, Three-quarters of a Sípára.
8. *Suls*, Three-quarters of a Sıpara.
9. *Sıpára*,[20] the Persian for the Arabic *Juz*. The Sípáras or Juz, are thirty in number, and it is said that the Qurán is so divided to enable the pious Muslim to recite the whole of the Qurán in the thirty days of Ramazán. Muhammadans generally quote their Qurán by the *Sıpara* and *Ruku'*, and not by the *Sura* and *A'yat*.
10. *Manzil* (pl. *manázil*), Stages. These are seven in number, and are marked by the letters F, M, Y, B, Sh, W, and Q, which words are said to spell *Famıbeshauq*, *i.e.*, "My mouth with desire." They have been arranged to enable the devout Muslim to recite the whole in the course of a week.

'Ilm-i-Usul,[21] or the Exegesis of the Qurán, is a science, some knowledge of which is absolutely necessary to enable the Christian controversialist to meet a Muhammadan opponent.

The words (*alfáz*) of the Qurán are of four classes:— *Khass, 'Amm, Mushtarak,* and *Muawwal*.

1. *Kháss*, Words used in a special sense. These are of three kinds:— *Khusús-ul-jins,* Special genus; *Khusús-un-nau'*, Special species; *Khusús-ul'-ain*, Special individuality.
2. *'Amm*, Collective or common, which embrace many individuals or things.

3. *Mushtarak*, Complex words which have several significations; *e.g. 'ain*, a word which signifies an Fye, a Fountain, the Knee, or the Sun.
4. *Muawwal*, Words which require to be explained: *e.g. Sulát* may mean either the Liturgical daily prayer (*Namáz*), or simple prayer (*Duá'*).

II. The Sentences (*'Ibárat*) of the Qurán are either *Záhir* or *Khafí*, *i.e.*, either Obvious or Hidden.

Obvious sentences are of four classes:— *Záhir*, *Nass, Mufassar, Muhkam.*

1. *Záhir*.—Those sentences, the meaning of which is *Obvious* or clear, without any assistance from the context (*karína*).
2. *Nass.*—Those sentences the meaning of which is *Manifest* from the text: e.g. "Take in marriage of such other women as please you, two, three, or four." Here it is manifest that the expression "such other women as please you" is restricted.
3. *Mufussar*:—Sentences which are *explained* by some expression in the verse: *e.g.* "And the angles prostrated themselves all of them with one accord *save Iblís*". Here it is explained that Iblís did not prostrate himselı.
4. *Mukham.*—Perspicuous sentences, the meaning of which is inconvertible: *e.g.* Súra-i-Máida (v.), 98, "He (God) knoweth all things."

Hidden sentences are either *Khají, Mushkil, Mujmal,* or *Mutashábih.*

1. *Khají.*—Sentences in which other persons or things are hidden beneath the plain meaning of a word or expression contained therein: e.g. Súra-i-Maida (v), 42, "As for a thief whether male or

female cut ye off their hands in recompense for their doings." In this sentence the word *Sáriq*, "thief," is understood to have *hidden* beneath its literal meaning, both pickpockets and highway robbers.

2. *Mushkil.*—Sentences which are *ambiguous*: *e.g.*, Súra-i-Dahr (lxxvi.), 15, "Vessels of silver and decanters which are of glass, decanters of glass with silver whose measure they shall mete."
3. *Mujmal.*—Sentences which are *compendious*, and have many interpretations : *e.g.*, Súra-i-Má'rij (lxx.), 19, "Man truly is by creation hasty."
4. *Mutashábih.*—*Intricate* sentences, or expressions, the exact meaning of which it is impossible for man to ascertain until the day of resurrection, but which was known to the Prophet: *e.g.*, the letters Alif, Lám, Mím (A.L.M.); Alif, Lám, Rá (A L.R.); Alif, Lám, Mím, Rá (A.L.M.R.), etc., at the commencement of different Súras or chapters. Also Súra-i-Mulk (lxvii.) 1, "In whose hand is the Kingdom," *i.e.*, God's *hand* (Arabic, *gad*); and Súra-i-Twá Há (xx.), "He is most merciful and sitteth on His throne," *i.e.*, God *sitteth* (Arabic, *istawá*); and Súra-i-Baqr (ii.), 115, "The face of God" (Arabic, *waj-ullah*).

III. The use (*isti'mál*) of words in the Qurán is divided into four classes. They are either *Haqíqat*, *Majaz, Saríh*, or *Kináyah*.

1. *Haqíqat.*—Words which are used in their *literal* meaning: *e.g.*, *rukú*, a prostration; *ziná*, adultery.
2. *Majáz.*—Words which are *figurative.*
3. *Saríh.*—Words the meaning of which is *clear* and

palpable; *e.g.*, "Thou art *free,*" "Thou art *divorced.*"

4. *Kináyah.*—Words which are *metaphorical* in their meaning: *e.g.*, "Thou art *separated*"; by which may be meant "thou art *divorced.*"

IV. The deduction of arguments, or *istidlál*, as expressed in the Qurán, is divided into four sections: *'Ibárat, Ishárat, Dalálat*, and *Iqtizá*.

1. *'Ibárat.*—The plain sentence.
2. *Ishárat.*—A sign or hint: *e.g.*, "Born of him;" meaning, of course, the father.
3. *Dalálat.*—The *argument* arising from a word or expression: *e.g.*, Súra-i-Baní Isráíl (xvii.), 23, "Say not unto your parents fie" (Arabic, *uff*); from which it is argued that children are not either to abuse or beat their parents.
4. *Iqtiza.*—*Demanding* certain conditions: *e.g.*, Súra-i-Nisá (iv.), 91, "Whoso killeth a Mumin (believer) by mischance shall be bound to free a slave." Here the condition demanded is that the slave shall be the property of the person who frees him.

An acquaintance with the use of these expressions used in the exegetical commentaries of the Qurán is of great assistance to the Bazaar-preacher, for it often happens that Maulavís interrupt the preacher by putting some difficult question, which the most able missionary will find it difficult to answer to the satisfaction of a mixed assemblage. For instance, an interesting discourse or discussion is often interrupted by a Maulaví putting the following question: "What did Jesus mean when He said, 'All that ever came before me were thieves or robbers?' " The best reply to such an one would be, "Maulaví Sáhib, you know, sentences are Záhir or Khafí, hidden or evident.

That is Khafí. Hidden sentences you know are of four kinds, Khafi, Mushkil, Mujmal, or Mutashábih. I consider the text you have quoted to be Mujmal, and you must admit that it would take up too much time to explain a *Mujmal* sentence in the midst of my present discourse." Most probably the Maulaví will be satisfied, for the preacher has applied a little flattering unction, in supposing that the Maulaví is learned in the principles of exegesis.

It is often painful to observe how some of our native preachers will attempt to explain the sacred mysteries of our faith in the midst of an ignorant mob. Whereas learned Muslim doctors, if placed in the same position, would decline to discuss mysterious questions under such conditions. They would say, as the Christian Divine might also say, "Many things in God's word are hidden (*khafí*), and cannot be explained to such a mixed audience as this, and besides this, in speaking of the nature (*zát*) of God, there is always some fear of blasphemy (*kufr*); I prefer speaking to you on that subject alone, after the preaching is over."

Some passages of the Qurán are contradictory, and are often made the subject of attack; but it is part of the theological belief of the Muslim doctor that certain passages of the Qurán are *mansúkh*, or abrogated by verses afterwards revealed. This was the doctrine taught by the Arabian prophet in the Súra-i-Baqr (ii.), 105, "Whatever verses we (*i.e.* God) cancel or cause thee to forget, we bring a better or its like." This convenient doctrine fell in with that law of expediency which appears to be the salient feature in Muhammad's prophetical career.

In the Tafsír-i-'Azízí it is written, that abrogated (*mansúkh*) verses of the Qurán are of three kinds : (1) Where the verse has been removed from the Qurán and another given in its place; (2) Where the injunction is abrogated and the letters of the verse remain; (3) Where both the verse and its injunction are removed from the text. This is also the view of Jalál-ud-Dín, who says, that the number of abrogated verses has been variously estimated from five to five hundred, and he gives the following Table of twenty verses which most commentators acknowledge to be abrogated, or *mansúkh*, with those verses which cancel them, or are *Násikh.*[22]

No.	*Mansukh*	*Násikh*	*Subject*
1.	Súra-i-Baqr (ii.), 115,	Sura-i-Baqr (ii.). 145,	The Qibla.
2.	Súra-i-Baqr (ii.), 178,	Śura-i-Máida (iv.), 49 Súra-i-Baní Israíl (xvii.), 35,	Qisás, or Relation.
3.	Súra-i-Baqr (ii.), 183,	Súra-i-Baqr (ii.), 187,	The Fast of Ramazán.
4.	Súra-i-Baqr (ii.), 184,	Súra-i-Baqr (ii.), 185	Fidya, or Expiation.
5.	Súra-i-Al-i-'Imrán (iii.), 102,	Súra-i-Taghábun (lxiv.), 16,	The fear of God.
6.	Súra-i-Niśa (iv.), 88,	Sura-i-Nisá (iv.), 89, Súra-i-Tauba (ix.), 5,	Jihád, or war with infidels.
7.	Súra-i-Baqr (ii.), 216	Súra-i-Tauba (ix.), 36	Jihád in the Sacred months.
8.	Súra-i-Baqr (ii.), 240,	Súra-i-Baqr (ii.), 234,	Provision for widows.
9.	Sura-i-Baqr (ii.), 191,	Súra-i-Tauba (ix.), 5,	Slaying enemies in the Sacred Mosque.
10.	Súra-í-Niśa (iv.), 14,	Súra-i-Núr (xxiv.), 2,	Imprisonment of the adulteress.
11.	Súra-i-Máida (v.), 105,	Sura-i-Taláq (lxv.), 2,	Witnesses
12.	Súra-i-Anfál (vii.), 66,	Súra-i-Anfál (vii.), 67,	Jihád, or war with infidels.
13.	Súra-i-Núr (xxiv), 3,	Súra-i-Núr (xxiv.), 32,	The marriage of adulterers.

Contd..

No.	*Mansukh*	*Násikh*	*Subject*
14.	Súra-i-Ahzáb (xxxiii.), 52,	Súra-i-Ahzáb (xxxiii.), 49,	The Prophet's wives.
15.	Súra-i-Mujádila (lviii.), 13, first part of verse.	Súra-i-Mujádila (lviii.), 13, latter part of verse.	Giving alms before assembling a council.
16.	Súra-i-Mumtahina (lx.), 11,	Súra-i-Tauba (ix.), 1,	Giving money to infidels for women taken in marriage.
17.	Súra-i-Tauba (ix.), 39,	Súra-i-Tauba (ix.), 92,	Jihád, or war with infidels.
18.	Súra-i-Muzammil (lxxiii.), 2,	Súra-i-Muzammil (lxxiii.), 20,	The night prayer.
19.	Súra-i-Núr (xxiv.), 57,	Súra-i-Núr (xxiv.), 58,	Permission to young children to enter a house.
20.	Súra-i-Nisá (iv.), 7,	Súra-i-Nisá (iv.), 11,	Division of property.

Upon a careful perusal of the Qurán, it does not appear that Muhammad ever distinctly declared that it was the object of his mission either to abrogate or to destroy the teaching of the previous prophets. On the contrary, we are told that the Qurán is "A book *confirmatory* of the previous Scriptures and their *safeguard.*"[23]

The Titles of the Chapters of the Quran

No.	*Title of Súra*	*Meaning in English.*	*The Chronological Order*		
			According to Jalál--uddín	*According to Rev. J.M. Rodwell*	*According to Sir W. Muir*
(1)	*(2)*	*(3)*	*(4)*	*(5)*	*(6)*
1.	Fátiha	Preface	uncertain	8	6
2.	Baqr	Cow	86	91	uncertain
3.	A'l-i-'Imrán	Family of Imrán	88	97	A.H. 2 to 10
4.	Nisá	Women	91	100	uncertain
5.	Máida	Table	112	114	A.H. 6 to 10

Contd..

(1)	(2)	(3)	(4)	(5)	(6)
6.	Anám	Cattle	54	89	81
7.	'Aráf	Aráf	38	87	91
8.	'Anfál	Spoils	87	95	A.H. 2
9.	Tauba	Repentance	113	113	The last
10.	Yúnus	Jonah	50	84	79
11.	Húd	Hud	51	75	78
12.	Yúsuf	Joseph	52	77	77
13.	R'ad	Thunder	95	90	89
14.	Ibráhím	Abraham	71	76	80
15.	Hajr	Hajr	53	57	62
16.	Nahl	Bee	69	73	88
17.	Baní Isráil	Children of Israel	49	67	87
18.	Kahaf	Cave	68	69	69
19.	Maryam	Mary	43	58	68
20.	Twá Há	Twá Há	44	55	75
21.	Ambiyá	Prophets	72	65	86
22.	Hajj	Pilgrimage	103	107	85
23.	Múminúm	Believers	73	64	84
24.	Núr	Light	102	105	A.H. 5
25.	Furqán	Qurán	41	66	74
26.	Sh'urá	Poets	46	56	61
27.	Namal	Ant	47	68	70
28.	Qasas	Story	48	79	83
29.	'Ankabút	Spider	84	81	90
30.	Rúm	Greeks	83	74	60
31.	Luqmán	Luqmán	56	82	50
32.	Sijda	Prostration	74	70	44
33.	Ahzáb	Confederates	89	103	uncertain
34.	Sabá	Saba	57	85	49
35.	Maláika	Angels	42	86	66
36.	Yá Sin	Yá Sín	40	60	67
37.	Sáffát	Ranks	55	50	59
38.	Swád	Swád	37	59	73

Contd..

(1)	(2)	(3)	(4)	(5)	(6)
39.	Zamár	Troops	58	80	45
40.	Múmin	Believer	59	78	72
41.	Fussilat	Explanation	60	71	53
42.	Shori	Council	61	83	71
43.	Zukhráf	Jewels	62	61	76
44.	Dukhán	Smoke	63	53	58
45.	Jâsiya	Kneeling	64	72	57
46.	Ahqáf	Ahqáf	65	88	64
47.	Muhammad	Muhammad	94	96	uncertain
48.	Fatah	Victory	111	108	A.H. 6
49.	Hujrát	Chambers	106	112	uncertain
50.	Qâf	Qaf	33	54	56
51.	Záriát	Breath of Winds	66	43	63
52.	Túr	Mountain	75	44	55
53.	Najam	Star	22	46	43
54.	Qamar	Moon	36	49	48
55.	Rahmán	Merciful	96	48	40
56.	Wáqia'	Inevitable	45	45	41
57.	Hadid	Iron	93	99	uncertain
58.	Mujádila	Disputer	105	106	uncertain
59.	Hashar	Assembly	101	102	A.H. 4
60.	Mumtahiná	Proof	90	110	A.H. 7
61.	Saf	Array	110	98	uncertain
62.	Jum'a	Assembly	108	94	uncertain
63.	Munáfiqún	Hypocrites	104	104	A.H. 65
64.	Taghábun	Deceit	109	93	82
65.	Taláq	Divorce	108	101	uncertain
66.	Tahrim	Prohibition	107	109	A.H. 7 to 8
67.	Mulk	Kingdom	76	63	42
68.	Qalam	Pen	2	17	52
69.	Háqa	Inevitable-Day	77	42	51
70.	Ma'árij	Steps	78	47	37
71.	Núh	Noah	70	51	54
72.	Jinn	Genii	39	62	65

Contd..

(1)	(2)	(3)	(4)	(5)	(6)
73.	Muzzammil	Wrapped up	3	3	46
74.	Muddassir	Mantle	4	2	21
75.	Qiyámat	Resurrection	30	40	36
76.	Dahr	Man	97	52	35
77.	Mursalát	Messengers	32	36	34
78.	Nabá	News	79	37	33
79.	Názi'át	Ministers of Vengeance	80	35	47
80.	'Abas	He frowned	23	24	26
81.	Takwir	Folding up	6	32	27
82.	Infitár	Cleaving asunder	81	31	11
83.	Tatfif	Short Measure	85	41	32
84.	Inshiqáq	Rending in sunder	82	33	28
85.	Burú	Celestial Signs	26	28	31
86.	Táriq	Night Star	35	22	29
87.	'A'la	Most High	7	25	23
88.	Gháshiya	Overwhelming	67	38	25
89.	Fajr	Day-break	9	39	14
90.	Balad	City	34	18	15
91.	Shams	Sun	25	23	4
92.	Lail	Night	8	16	12
93.	Zuhá	Sun in his meridian	10	4	16
94.	Inshiráh	Expanding	11	5	17
95.	Tín	Fig	27	26	8
96.	'Alaq	Congealed blood	1	1	19
97.	Qadar	Night of power	24	92	24
98.	Baiyana	Evidence	99	21	uncertain
99.	Zilzál	Earthquake	92	30	3
100.	'Adiyát	Swift horses	13	34	2
101.	Qári'a	Striking	29	29	7
102.	Takásur	Multiplying	15	15	9

Contd..

(1)	(2)	(3)	(4)	(5)	(6)
103.	'Asar	Afternoon	12	27	1
104.	Hamza	Slanderer	31	13	10
105.	Fil	Elephant	18	19	13
106.	Qoreish	Qoreish	28	20	5
107.	Máún	Necessaries	16	14	39
108.	Kausar	Kausar	14	9	18
109.	Kafirún	Infidels	17	12	38
110.	Nasr	Assistance	101	111	30
111.	Lahab	Lahab	5	11	22
112.	Ikhlás	Unity	21	10	20
113.	Falaq	Day-break	19	6	uncertain
114.	Nás	Men	20	7	uncertain

It must be admitted that the Qurán deserves the highest praise for its conception of the Divine nature and that it embodies much deep and noble earnestness.

References

1. The contents of this article appear as an Introduction to the Roman-Urdú edition of the Qurán, published at Ludianah, North India, 1877.
2. According to Jalál-ud-dín Syuty there are fifty-five titles of the Qurán. (See the Itqán, p. 117).
3. See Jalál-ud-dín's Itqán, p. 91. The "Recording Angels" mentioned in the Súra-i-Abas (lxxx.), 15, are said to have written the Qurán before it was sent down from heaven.
4. Gabriel (*Jibráíl*) is only mentioned twice by name in the Qurán: once in the verse noted above, and again in the Súra-i-Tahrím (lxvi.), 4. He is supposed to be alluded to under the title of Rúh-ul-Qudus, or the Holy Spirit, in Súras Baqr (ii.), 82, 254; Máida (v.), 109; Nahl (xvi.), 104.
5. *Malak*. Hebrew, *Malakh*, an angel; prophet; a name of office, not of nature. See Wilson's Hebrew Lexicon, p. 13.
6. Mishkat, bk. xxiv. chap. v. pt. 1.
7. Capt. Matthews, in his edition of the Mishkát, has followed the Persian Commentator, and translated the word *Malak*, Gabriel, instead of Angel, and most of our English authors have quoted the tradition from his book.

8. Súra-i-Alaq (xcvi.), the first five verses. The other verses of the chapter are of a later date.

9. *Námús*. Understood by all Commentators to be the angel Gabriel. It has, however, many significations, *e.g.,* Law, Voice, Sound, & c. (see Johnson's Arabic Dictionary). Probably a corruption of the Greek *νόμος*, which is always used in the New Testament for the Law of Moses.

10. The ancient Jews divided the whole Law of Moses into fifty-four Sections, which were called *Sidrah*, or an order or division. These sections had each a technical name, *e.g.,* the first was called "Bereshith," and the second "Naoh." (See Dr. Adam Clark on Genesis).

11. Mishkát, bk. viii. chap. iii. pt. 3.

12. Muir's "Life of Mohamet," vol. i. Introduction.

13. See the Hyát-ul-Kalúb, a Shi'ah book of Traditions, leaf 420. "The Ansárs were ordained to oppose the claims of the family of Muhammad, and this was the reason why the other wretches took the office of Khalif by force. After thus treating one Khalif of God, they then mutilated and changed the other Khalif, which is the book of God."

14. Mishkát, bk. ii., chap. ii., pt. 1.

15. Abdul Haqq, the Persian Commentator of the Mishkát.

16. The chronological list as given in Jalál-ud-dín Syuty's Itqán will be found in the Index of the Súras.

17. See Rodwell's Introduction to the English Qurán, in which the Súras are chronologically arranged.

18. See a book by M. Geiger entitled, "Was hat Muhammad aus dem Judenthume aufgenommen," in which that learned Jew has traced all the leading features of Islám to Talmudic sources. Also "Literary Remains of Emanuel Deutsch." Essay on Islám.

19. Unfortunately the verses in Rodwell's English Quran do not correspond with the Arabic Qurāns in use amongst the Muhammadans of India.

20. The Persian word *Sipára* is derived from *sí*, thirty, and *pára*, a portion.

21. 'Ilm-i-Usúl embraces both the exegesis of the Qurán and Hadís. The most authoritative works on the 'Ilm-i-Usúl of the Qurán are Syuty's Itqán (Sprenger's edition), and the Manor-ul-Usúl, and its commentary the Núr-ul-Anwár.

22. It is to be regretted that the Greed verb καταλύω, in St. Matthew, v. 17, has been translated in some of the versions of the New Testament by *mansúkh*; for it gives rise to needless controversy, and conveys a wrong impression to the Muhammadan mind as to the Christian view regarding this question. According to most Greek lexicons, the Greek word means to *throw down*, or to *destroy* (as of a building), which is the meaning given to the word in our authorised English translation. Christ did not come to destroy, or to pull down, the Law and the Prophets; but we all admit that certain precepts of the Old Testament were abrogated by those of the new Testament. Indeed we further admit that the old covenant was abrogated by the new covenant of grace. "He taketh away the first that he may establish the second." Heb. x. 9.

In the Arabic translation of the New Testament, printed at Beyrut, A.D. 1869, καταλύω is translated by *naqz*, "to de-molish"; and in Mr. Loewenthal's Pashto translation, A.D. 1863, by *bátildwal*, "to destroy," or "render void,"; and in Henry Martyn's Persian Testament, A.D. 1837, it is also translated by the Arabic *ibtál*. *i.e.,* "making void." In both the Arabic-Urdú and Roman-Urdú it is unfortunately rendered *mansúkh*, a word which has a technical meaning in Muhammadan theology contrary to that implied in the word used by our Lord in Matthew, v. 17.

23. Sura-i-Máida (v.), 52.

24. Sura-i-Baqr (ii.), 136; also Sura-i-A'l-i-'Imran (iii.), 83.

5
Inspiration

According to Muhammadan theologians, inspiration is of two kinds, *Wáhí* and *Ilhám. Wáhi*, is that which was given to the prophets, and is used especially for the Qurán; *Ilhám* being the inspiration to *Walis*, or saints.

Ilhám is the word generally used by Christian missionaries for the inspiration of the sacred Scriptures, and we believe it is sometimes used by Arabic divines for a higher form of inspiration, but always in the compound form of *Ilhám Rabbáni.*

Shaikh Ahmad in his book, the Núr-ul-Anwár, defines inspiration as follows:— "*Wáhí*, or inspiration, is either *Záhir* (external), or *Bátin* (internal). *Wáhí Záhir* is divided into three classes:— (1) *Wáhí Qurán*, that which was given by the mouth of the angel Gabriel, and which reached the ear of the Prophet after he knew that it was Gabriel who spoke to him. (2) *Ishárat-ul-Malak*, that which was received from Gabriel, but not by word of mouth, as when the Prophet said, 'The Holy Ghost has breathed into my heart.' (3) *Ilhám*, or *Wáhí Qalb*, that which was made known to the Prophet by the light of prophecy. This kind of inspiration is possessed by Walis or saints, but in their case it may be true or false. *Wáhí Bátin* is that which the Prophet obtained by analogical reasoning (*qiás*) just as the enlightened doctors, or *Muftahidín*, obtain it."

The *Ishárat-ul-Malak*, mentioned in the above quotation is never used for the inspiration of the Qurán, but for certain instructions which Muhammad professes to have received direct from Gabriel, and which are recorded in the *Hadís*, or Traditions.

Whatever may have been the actual impression upon Muhammad's mind as to the nature of the communications he professed to have received from God, it is evident that Muslim theologians have no conception of the World of God being given in the form of the Old and New Testament Scriptures. The most plausible objection raised against the New Testament, by Muhammadan controversialists of the present day, is that the Christians have lost the original Gospels and that our present book contains merely the *Hadís* or traditions, of Matthew, Mark, Luke, and John. It is, therefore, necessary to correct their common idea that the Gospel was revealed to Jesus in the same manner as the Qurán is said to have been given to Muhammad; to show that it was the special office of the Holy Spirit to give the New Testament Scriptures, and that they came to man by the same method of inspiration whereby the Old Testament writings were given to the Prophets of old, the Qurán being an exception to God's *usual* method of giving inspired writings to his Prophets.[1]

Reference

1. *Vide* 2 Tim. iii. 16 : *πᾶσα γραφὴ Θεόπνευστος* "all scripture is God-breathed" (*divinatus inspirata,* Vulg.), which Dean Alford says is the idea common to the Jews. *Vide* Jos. contra Apion. i. 7.

6
The Traditions

The *Hadís* (pl. *Ahádís*) is, as we have already remarked, the second part of the Muhammadan rule of faith. It forms the body of that oral law of the Arabian legislator which stands next to the Qurán in point of authority, being considered by all Muhammadans, whether Sunní, Shía'h, or Wahhábi, as a supplement to that book. The collections of these traditions are called *Hadís*, being records of the saying of the Prophet, but they are also called *Sunna*, a word which signifies custom, or regulation.

Muhammad gave very special injunctions respecting the faithful transmission of his sayings; for example, it is related by Tirmizi, that the Prophet said, "Convey to other persons none of my words except those which ye know of a surety. Verily he who purposely represents my words wrongly, would find a place nowhere for himself but in fire."

Abu Dáud received only four thousand eight hundred, out of five hundred thousand, and even after this *careful* selection he states that he has mentioned, "*those which seem to be authentic and those which are nearly so.*" Out of forty thousand persons who have been instrumental in handing down traditions of "the Prophet," Bokhárí only acknowledged two thousand as reliable authorities. Such being the case, it is not surprising that *'Ilm-i-Hadís*, or the Science of Tradition, has become a most important branch of Muslim Divinity, and that the following canons have been framed for the reception or rejection of traditions.

I. With reference to the character of those who have handed down the tradition[1]:—

1. *Hadís-i-Sahíh,* a *genuine* tradition, is one which has been handed down by truly pious persons who have been distinguished for their integrity.
2. *Hadís-i-Hasan,* a *mediocre* tradition, is one the narrators of which do not approach in moral excellence to those of the Sahíh class.
3. *Hadís-i-Z'aíf,* a *weak* tradition, is one whose narrators are of questionable authority.

The disputed claims of narrators to these three classes have proved a fruitful source of learned discussion, and very numerous are the works written upon the subject.

II.—With reference to the original relators of the Hadís:—

1. *Hadís-i-Marfu'*, an *exalted* tradition, is a saying, or an act, related or performed by the Prophet himself and handed down in a tradition.
2. *Hadís-i-Mauquf,* a *restricted* tradition, is a saying or an act related or performed by one of the *asháb* or companions of the Prophet.
3. *Hadís-i-Máqtu'*, an *intersected* tradition, is a saying or an act related or performed by one of the *Tába'ín*, or those who conversed with the companions of the Prophet.

III.—With reference to the links in the chain of the narrators of the tradition, a Hadís is either *Muttasil*, connected, or *Munqata'*, disconnected. If the chain of narrators is complete from the time of the first utterance of the saying or performance of the act recorded to the time that it was written down by the collector of traditions, it is *Muttasil*; but if the chain of narrators is incomplete, it is *Munqata.*'

IV.—With reference to the manner in which the tradition has been narrated, and transmitted down from the first:—

1. *Hadís-i-Mutawátir*, an *undoubted* tradition, is one which is handed down by very many distinct chains of narrators, and which has been always accepted as authentic and genuine, no doubt ever having been raised against it. The learned doctors say there are only five such traditions; but the exact number is disputed.
2. *Hadís-i-Mashúr,* a *well-known* tradition, is one which has been handed down by at least three distinct lines of narrators. It is called also *Mustafíz*, diffused. It is also used for a tradition which was at first recorded by one person, or a few individuals, and afterwards became a popular tradition.
3. *Hadís-i-'Azír*, a *rare* tradition, is one related by only two lines of narrators.
4. *Hadís-i-Gharíb*, a *poor* tradition, is one related by only one line of narrators.

Khabar-i-Wáhid, a *single saying*, is a term also used for a tradition related by one person and handed down by one line of narrators. It is a disputed point whether a *Khabar-i-Wáhid* can form the basis of Muslim doctrine.

Hadís-i-Mursal (lit. "a tradition let loose"), is a tradition which any collector of traditions such as Bokhári and others, records with the assertion, "*the Apostle of God said*".

Riwáyat, is a Hadís which commences with the words "*it is related,*" without the authority being given.

Hadís-i-Mauzu', an *invented* tradition, is one the *untruth* of which is beyond dispute.

It is an universal cannot that no tradition can be received which is contrary to the Qurán, and it is related that when 'Ayeshah heard Omar say that Muhammad had taught that the dead could hear, she rejected the tradition as spurious, because it was contrary to the teaching of the Qurán.

Whatever may be the difference of opinion as to the authority of the various traditions, it must be remembered that they form the groundwork of the different schools of thought of the Muhammadan religion. It is, therefore, impossible for European critics to form a just estimate of the Muhammadan creed without being acquainted with those traditions which are generally received as authentic and genuine.

European writers are unfortunately under the impression that the "Muhammadan revival" is a going back to "first principles," as expressed in the Qurán, whereas, it is, as we have already remarked, a revival of the study of the traditions concerning their Prophet, which study has undoubtedly been promoted by the establishment of printing presses in Egypt, Turkey, and India. Not that we think Islám will present any fairer proportions even when deprived of those excrescences which are supposed to have been the preternatural growth of tradition, as long as the Pilgrimage has the so-called divine sanction of the Qurán, and the position of women is regulated by the same "divine oracles."

The following are the six principal collectors of Hadís received by the Sunni Muhammadans :—

1. Muhammad Ismail *Bokhári.*[2]

Born, A.H. 194; died, A.H. 256.

2. *Muslim-ibn-i-Hajjáj.*

Born, A.H. 204; died, A.H. 261.

3. Abu Isa' Muhammad *Tirmızí.*

Born, A.H. 209; died, A.H. 279.

4. *Abu Dáud* Sajistaní.

Born, A.H. 202; died, A.H. 275.

5. Abu Abdur Rahmán *Nasaí.*

Born, A.H. 215; died, A.H. 303.

6. Abu Abdullah Muhammad *Ibn-i-Májah.*

Born, A.H. 209; died, A.H. 273.

Some divines substitute the following for that of *Ibn-i-Májah.*

Muawattáa Imám Málik.

Born, A.H. 95; died, A.H. 179.

The following are the collections of Hadís received by the Shía'h:—

1. The *Káfi*, by Abu Jáfar Muhamad, A.H. 329.
2. The *Man-lá-yastahzirah-al-Faqih* by Shekh 'Ali, A.H. 381.
3. The *Tahzıb*, by Shekh Abu Jáfar Muhammad, A.H. 466.
4. The *Istibsár*, by the same author.

5. The *Nahaj-ul-Balághat*, by Sayyud Razi, A.H. 406.

Copies of the *Sihah-Sittah*, or "six correct" books of tradition received by the Sunnís, together with the seventh work by Imám Málik, have been lithographed, and can be purchased in the book shops of Delhi, Lucknow, and Bombay; but the work most read is the Mishkát-ul-Musábíh (the niche for lamps), which is a collection of the most reliable traditions. This work was originally in Arabic; but it was translated into Persian in the reign of Akbar. It was rendered into English by Captain Matthews, and published in Calcutta in 1809. The English translation has been long since out of print, but efforts are being made by the author of these notes for its republication. The popular collection of Shía'h traditions arranged in the form of an historical narrative is the Hyát-ul-Qulub, a Persian work which has been translated by the Rev. J.L. Merrick (Phillips, Sampson, and Co., Boston, U.S., 1850).

The most trustworthy of the various collections of Sunni traditions is the one usually called *Bokhárí*. It was compiled by Abu Abdullah Muhammad ibn-i-Ismaíl a native of Bokhára. In obedience to instructions he is said to have received in a vision, he set himself to commence the collection of all the current traditions relating to Muhammad. He succeeded in collecting not fewer than six hundred thousand traditions, of which he selected only 7225 as trustworthy! These he recorded in his work; but it is said that he repeated a two *rik'at* prayer before he wrote down any one of the 7275 traditions which he recorded. There is, therefore, every reason to believe that the compilers of the books of tradition were sincere and honest in their endeavours to produce correct and well authenticated traditions of their Prophet's precepts and practice; but, as Sir William Muir remarks, "The exclusively oral character of the early traditions deprives them of every check against the licence of error and fabrication."

But although the traditions of Muhammad are shrouded with a degree of uncertainty which is perplexing, to the student of history, still there can be no doubt as to the place they were intended to, and still do occupy in the theological structure of Islám. And everything Muhammad said with reference to religious dogmas and morals is believed to have been inspired by God; by a "*wáhí ghair-i-mutlu*'," or an inspiration similar in kind to that which we believe to have been given to the inspired writers of our Christian Scriptures.

References

1. In the first edition of these Notes the canons for the reception and rejection of traditions were taken from Sayyad Ahmad Khan's "Essay on Traditions," but in the present edition they have been arranged according to the Arabic treatise, entitled Nukhbat-al-Faqr, by Shekh Shaháb-ud-dín Ahmad, edited by Capt. W. Nassau Lees, L.L.D. (Calcutta, 1862).
2. The names in *italics* denotes the usual title of the book.

7
Ijma'

Ijma' is the third foundation of the Muhammadan rule of faith. It literally means *collecting,* or *assembling*, and in Muslim divinity it expresses the unanimous consent of the Mujtahidín (learned doctors); or, as we should call it, "the unanimous consent of the Fathers." A Mujtahid is a Muslim divine of the highest degree of learning, a title usually conferred by Muslim rulers. There are three foundations of *Ijma'*: (1) *Itifáq-i-Qauli*, unanimous consent expressed in declaration of *opinion*; (2) *Itifáq-i-Fi'li*, expressed in unanimity of *practice*; (3) *Itifáq-i-Saqúti*, when the majority of the Mujtahidín signified their tacit assent to the opinions of the minority by "*silence*" or non-interferance.

The Mujtahidín, capable of making *Ijma'*, must be "men of learning and piety, not heretics, nor fools, but men of judgment."

There is great diversity of opinion as to up to what period in the history of Islám, *Ijma'* can be accepted. Some doctors assert that only the *Ijma'* of the Mujtahidín who were Asháb (companions); others, that of those who were not only "companions" but "descendants" of the "Prophet," can be accepted; whilst others accept the *Ijma'* of the *Ansars*, (helpers,) and of the *Muhájarín* (fugitives,) who were dwellers in Medina with Muhammad. The majority of learned Muslim divines, however, appear to think that *Ijma'* may be collected in every age, although they admit that owing to the numerous divisions which have arisen amongst Muhammadans, it has not been possible since the days of the *Taba' Taba'ín*, (*i.e.,* the followers of the followers of the companions).

The following is considered to be the relative value of *Ijma'*:—

That of the *Asháb* (companions) is equal to *Hadís Muatwátir*. That which was decided afterwards, but in accordance with the unanimous opinion of the Asháb, is equal to *Hadís Khabar-i-Mashhúr*, and that upon which there was diversity of opinion amongst the *Asháb*, but has since been decided by the later Mujtahidín is equal to *Hadís-i-Khabar-i-Wáhid.*

Amongst the Shia'hs, we believe, there are still *Mujtahidín* whose *Ijma'* is accepted, but the Sunnís have four orthodox schools of interpretation, named after their respective founders, Hanafí, Sháfa'i, Máliki, and Hambali. The Wahhábis for the most part reject Ijma' collected after the death of "the Companions".

Reference

1. The seventy-three sects are, according to some writers, distributed as follows:— Shia'h 21, M'utazilah 21, Khawárij 7, Murjíah 5, Najáriah 3, Jabariyah 2, Mushabiyah 1, and Nájíah (the term used for the orthodox).

8
Qias

Qíás (lit. "to compare") is the fourth foundation of Islám, and expresses the analogical reasoning of the learned with regard to the teaching of the Qurán, Hadis, and Ijmá.

There are four conditions of Qíás: (1) That the precept or practice upon which it is founded must be of common (*'amm*) and not of special (*khâss*) application; (2) The cause (*illat*) of the injunction must be known and understood; (3) The decision must be based upon either the Qurán, the Hadís, or the Ijma'; (4) The decision arrived at must not be contrary to anything declared elsewhere in the Qurán and Hadís.

Qias is of two kinds, *Qíás-i-Jalí* or evident, and *Qíás-i-Khaji* or hidden.

An example of *Qíás-i-Jalí* is as follows:— Wine is forbidden in the Qurán under the word *Khamar,* which literally means anything intoxicating; it is, therefore, evident that opium and all intoxicating drugs are also forbidden. *Qíás-i-Khafí* is seen in the following example:— In the Hadís it is enjoined that one goat in forty must be given to God. I'o some poor persons the money may be more acceptable; therefore, the value of the goat may be given instead of the goat.

9
Faith

Faith, I'mán, is defined as "the belief of the heart and the confession of the mouth." It is of two kinds — *I'mán-i-Mujmal* and *I'mán-i-Mufassal*.

I'mán-i-Mujmal is a simple expression of faith in the teaching of the Qurán and the Hadís.

I'mán-i-Mufassal is a belief in the six articles of faith, *viz.*:— 1. The Unity of God. 2. The Angels. 3. The Books. 4. The Prophets. 5. The Day of Judgment. 6. Predestination, or the Decrees of God.

10
Allah or God

The name of the Creator of the universe in the Qurán is *Allah*, which is the title given to the Supreme Being by Muhammadans of every race and language. It is called the special, or essential, name of God, the *ism-i-zát*; all other names being considered merely *ism-i-safát*, or attributes, of which there are said to be ninety-nine.[1] It is supposed to have been derived from the word *iláh*, a deity or god, with the addition of the definite article *al*, thus *Al-ilah*. *The* God. But Imám Haníf́a says that, just as God's essence is unchangeable so is His name, and that *Alláh* has always been the name of the great Eternal Being (*vide* Ghyás-ul-Loghát). It appears to be an Arabic rendering of the Hebrew 98 *el,* God. It is expressed in Persian and Hindustani by the word *Khudá*, derived from the Persian *Khud* (*self*); the self-existing one.

The Muhammadan belief in the existence of God is expressed in the first part of the well known confession of faith, *La-iláha Il-lal-láho*, "There is no deity but God," the interpretation of which occupies so prominent a place in all treatises of divinity.

The following is an interpretation of the Muslim belief in the existence and nature of God, by the famous scholastic divine, Imám Ghazáli, in his book entitled Al Maqsud-ul-asná, an extract from which Ockley has translated from Pocock's Specimen Historiæ Arabum:—

"Praise be to God the Creator and Restorer of all things; who does whatsoever he pleases, who is Master of the glorious throne and mighty force, and directs his sincere servants into the right way and the straight path; who favoureth them, who have once borne testimony to the unity, by preserving their confessions from the darkness of doubt and hesitation; who directs them to follow his chosen apostle, upon whom be the blessing and peace of God; and to go after his most honourable companions, to whom he hath vouchsafed his assistance and direction which is revealed to them in his essence and operations by the excellencies of his attributes, to the knowledge whereof no man attains but he that hath been taught by hearing. To these, as touching his essence, he maketh known that he is one, and hath no partner; singular, without anything like him; uniform, having no contrary; separate, having no equal. He is ancient, having no first; eternal, having no beginning; remaining for ever, having no end; continuing to eternity, without any termination. He persists, without ceasing to be; remains without falling, and never did cease, nor ever shall cease to be described by glorious attributes, nor is subject to any decree so as to be determined by any precise limits or set times, but is the First and the Last, and is within and without.

"(*What God is not.*) He, glorified be his name, is not a body endued with form, nor a substance circumscribed with limits or determined by measure; neither does he resemble bodies, as they are capable of being measured or divided. Neither is he a substance, neither do substances exist in him; neither is he an accident, nor do accidents exist in him. Neither is he like to anything that exists, neither is anything like to him; nor is he determinate in quantity nor comprehended by bounds, nor circumscribed by the differences of situation, nor contained in the heavens. He sits upon the throne, after that manner which he himself hath described, and in that same sense which he himself means, which is a sitting far removed from any notion of contact, or resting upon, or local situation; but both the throne itself, and whatsoever is upon it, are sustained by the goodness of his power, and are subject to the grasp of his hand. But he is above the throne, and above all things, even to the utmost ends of the earth; but so above as at the same time not to be a whit nearer the throne and the heaven; since he is exalted by (infinite) degrees above the throne no less than he is exalted above the earth, and at the same time is near to everything that hath a being, nay, 'nearer to man than their jugular veins, and is witness to everything:'[2] though his nearness is not like the nearness of bodies, as neither is his essence like the essence of bodies. Neither both he exist in anything, neither doth anything exist in him; but he is too high to be contained in any place, and too holy to be determined by time; for he was before time and place were created, and is now after the same manner as he always was. He is also distinct from the creatures by his attributes, neither is there anything besides himself in his essence, nor is his essence in any other besides him. He is too holy to be subject to change, or any local motion; neither do any accidents dwell in him, nor any contingencies befall him; but he abides through all generations with his glorious attributes, free from all danger of dissolution. As to the attribute of perfection, he wants no addition of his perfection. As to being, he is known to exist by the apprehension of the understanding; and he is seen as he is by an ocular intuition, which will be vouchsafed out of his mercy and grace to the holy in the eternal mansion, completing their joy by the vision of his glorious presence.

"(*His Power.*) He, praised be his name, is living, powerful, mighty, omnipotent, not liable to any defect or impotence; neither slumbering nor sleeping, nor being obnoxious to decay or death. To him belongs the kingdom, and the power, and the might. His is the dominion, and the excellency, and the creation, and the command thereof. The heavens are folded up in his right hand, and all creatures are couched within his grasp. His excellency consists in his creating and producing, and his unity in communicating existence and a beginning of being. He created men and their works, and measured out their maintenance and their determined times. Nothing that is possible can escape his grasp, nor can the vicissitudes of things elude his power. The effects of his might are innumerable, and the objects of his knowledge infinite.

"(*His knowledge.*) He, praised be his name, knows all things that can be understood, and comprehends whatsoever comes to pass, from the extremities of the earth to the highest heavens. Even the weight of a pismire could not escape him either in earth in heaven; but he would perceive the creeping of the black pismire in the dark night upon the hard stone, and discern the motion of an atom in the open air. He knows what is secret and conceals it, and views the conceptions of the minds, and the motions of the thoughts, and the inmost recesses of secrets, by a knowledge ancient and eternal, that never ceased to be his attribute from eternal eternity, and not by any new knowledge, superadded to his essence, either inhering or adventitious.

"(*His will.*) He, praised be his name, doth will those things to be that are, and disposes of all accidents. Nothing passes in the empire, nor the kingdom, neither little nor much, nor small nor great, nor good nor evil, nor profitable nor hurtful, nor faith nor infidelity, nor knowledge nor ignorance, nor prosperity nor adversity, nor increase nor decrease, nor obedience nor rebellion, but by his determinate counsel and decree, and his definite sentence and will. Nor doth he wink of him that seeth, nor the subtlety of him that thinketh, exceed the bounds of his will; but it is he who gave all things their beginning; he is the creator and restorer, the sole operator of what he pleases; there is no reversing his decree nor delaying what he hath determined, nor is there any refuge to man from his rebellion against him, but only his help and mercy; nor hath any man any power to perform any duty towards him, but through his love and will. Though men, genii, angels and devils, should conspire together either to put one single atom in motion, or cause it to cease its motion, without his will and approbation they would not be able to do it. His will subsists in his essence amongst the rest of his attributes, and was from eternity one of his eternal attributes, by which he willed from eternity the existence of those things that he had decreed, which were produced in their proper reasons according to his eternal will, without any *before* or *after*, and in agreement both with his knowledge and will, and not by methodising of thoughts, nor waiting for a proper time, for which reason no one thing is in him a hindrance from another.

"(*His hearing and sight.*) And he, praised be his name, is hearing and seeing, and heareth and seeth. No audible object, how still soever, escapeth his hearing; nor is any thing visible so small as to escape his sight; for distance is no hindrance to his hearing, nor darkness to his sight. He sees without pupil or eyelids, and hears without any passage or ear, even as he knoweth without a heart, and performs his actions without the assistance of any corporeal limb, and creates without any instrument, for his attributes (or properties) are not like those of men any more than his essence is like theirs.

"(*His word.*) Furthermore, he doth speak, command, forbid, promise, and threaten by an eternal, ancient word, subsisting in his essence. Neither is it like to the word of the creatures, nor doth it consist in a voice arising from the commotion of the air and the collision of bodies, nor letters which are separated by the joining together of the lips of the motion of the tongue. The Koran, the Law, the Gospel, and the Pslater, are books sent down by him to his apostles, and the Koran, indeed, is read with tongues, written in books, and kept in hearts; yet as subsisting in the essence of God, it doth not become liable to separation and division whilst it is transferred into the hearts and the papers. Thus Moses also heard the Word of God without voice or letter, even as the saints behold the essence of God without substance or accident. And that since these are his attributes, he liveth and knoweth, is powerful and willeth and operateth, and seeth and speaketh, by life and knowledge, and will and hearing, and sight and word, not by his simple essence.

"(*His works.*) He, praised be his name, exists after such a manner that nothing besides him hath any being but what is produced by his operation, and floweth from his justice after the best, most excellent, most perfect, and most just model. He is, moreover, wise in his works, and just in his decrees. But his justice is not to be compared with the justice of men. For a man may be supposed to act unjustly by invading the possession of another; but no injustice can be conceived of God, inasmuch as there is nothing that belongs to any other besides himself, so that wrong is not imputable to him as meddling with things not appertaining to him. All things, himself only excepted, genii, men, the devil, angels, heaven, earth, animals, plants, substance, accident, intelligible, sensible, were all created originally by him. He created them by his power out of mere privation, and brought them into light, when as yet they were nothing at all, but he alone existing from eternity, neither was there any other with him. Now he created all things in the beginning for the manifestation of his power, and his will, and the confirmation of his word, which was true from all eternity. Not that he stood in need of them, nor wanted them; but he manifestly declared his glory in creating, and producing, and commanding, without being under any obligation, nor out of necessity. Loving kindness, and to show favour, and grace, and beneficence, belong to him; whereas it is in his power to pour forth upon men a variety of torments, and afflict them with various kinds of sorrows and diseases, which, if he were to do, his justice could not be arraigned, nor would he be chargeable with injustice. Yet he rewards those that worship him for their obedience on account of his promise and beneficence, not of their merit nor of necessity, since there is nothing which he can be tied to perform; nor can any injustice be supposed in him, nor can he be under any obligation to any person whatsoever. That his creatures, however, should be bound to serve him, ariseth from his having declared by the tongues of the prophets that it was due to him from them. The worship of him is not simply the dictate of the understanding, but he sent messengers to carry to men his commands, and promises, and threats, whose veracity he proved by manifest miracles, whereby men are obliged to give credit to them in those things that they relate."

References

1. *Vide* the ninety-nine names of God in the article on Zikr. There is also the *Ism-ul-'Azam*, the exalted name of God, which is said to be unknown.
2. *Vide* Qurán.

11
Angels

The existence of angels (*malak*, pl. *maláik*), and their purity, are absolutely required to be believed in by the Qurán, and he is reckoned an infidel who denies that there are such beings, or hates any of them or asserts any distinction of the sexes. The Muhammadans reckon four archangels: (1) *Jibráíl* (Gabriel), who is God's messenger; (2) *Míkáíl*, (Michael), who is the protector of the Jews; (3) *Isráfíl*, who will sound the last trumpet at the resurrection; (4) *Azráíl*, the angle of death. Muhammad undoubtedly obtained the names of these archangels from the Scriptures and Jewish tradition, although in the Apocryphal Book of Enoch[1] the names of the six archangels are *Uriel, Raphael, Raguel, Michael, Sarakiel, Gabriel* — a fact which may be cited as an additional proof, that Muhammad availed himself of Jewish traditions.

There are also the two recording angels called the *Mua'qqibát*, or the angels who continually succeed each other, who record the good and evil actions of a man, one standing at his right hand and another on his left. These are also called the *Kirám-ul-Kátibín* (the exalted writers). The angle who has charge of Heaven is *Rezwán* and the angle who presides over Hell is *Málik*.

Munkar and *Nakír* are described by Muhammad as two black angels with blue eyes who visit every man in his grave, make him sit up, and examine him as to his faith in God and in Muhammad his prophet. If the answer is satisfactory, he will be allowed to sleep on in peace, but if he replies that he knows nothing of "*God's Apostle,*" then he will be struck with an iron hammer called *Mitraqat*, and he will roar out, and his cries will be heard by all animals that may be near his grave, excepting men and genii.[2] This exciting ceremony is to take place as soon as the funeral party have proceeded forty paces from the grave![3]

The Devil is said to be a fallen angel who was turned out of Paradise because he refused to do homage to Adam.[4] He is called *Iblís*, a word which is most probably derived from *balas*, a wicked or profligate person; and also *Shaitán* (Satan). Besides angels and devils, there are said to be a distinct order of creatures called *Jinn* (Genii) who were created of fire some thousands of years before Adam. According to tradition the species consists of five distinct orders:—1. *Jánn*; 2. *Jinn*; 3. *Shaitán*; 4. *'Ifrít; 5. Márid.*

Their chief abode is the mountains of Qáf, which are supposed to encircle the world.

There are good and evil Genii. If good, they are exceedingly handsome; if evil, they are horribly hideous. The evil genii are said to have been at liberty to enter any of the seven heavens till the birth of Jesus, when they were excluded from three of them. On the birth of Muhammad they were forbidden the other four heavens. They continue, however, to ascend to the confines of the lowest heavens, and there listen to the conversations of the angels respecting the decrees of God, which they sometimes impart to men by means of talismans and invocations.

The good genii are Muslims, and perform all the religious duties of the faithful.

King Solomon is said to have had great power over the genii by means of his magic ring.[5]

Students of Islam must bear in mind that most of the stories of the genii are related in the Qurán, and have, therefore, received from Muhammad all the authority of a divine revelation.

References

1. Book of Enoch translated by Archbishop Laurence, chap. xx.
2. Mishkát, bk. i. chap. v.
3. *Vide* Article on Janaza or Burial.
4. Surat-ul-Baqr, 33.
5. The second Targum on Esther i.—ii., mentions the four classes of Genii which were given into the power of King Solomon.

12
Prophets

The number of prophets (*rasúl*), which have been sent by God, are said to be 224,000, or, according to another tradition, 124,000. Of these 313 were Apostles sent with special commissions, to reclaim the world from infidelity and superstition.

Six brought new laws which successively abrogated the preceding and have special titles, or *kalima*[1] :—

1. *Adam* (Adam), *Sufi-Ullah,* the Chosen of God.
2. *Nuh* (Noah), *Nabi-Ullah,* the Preacher of God.
3. *Ibrahím* (Abraham), *Khalíl-Ullah*, the Friend of God.
4. *Musá* (Moses), *Kalim-Ullah*, one who conversed with God.
5. *'Isa* (Jesus), *Ruh Ullah*, the Spirit of God.
6. Muhammad, *Rusúl-Ullah*, the Messenger of God.

The number of sacred books delivered to man are said to have been one hundred and four, viz. :—

Ten, to Adam;

Fifty, to Seth (*Sísh*);

Thirty, to Enoch (*Edrís*);

Ten, to Abraham;

The Taurát, to Moses;

The Zabur, to David,

The Injíl, to Jesus;

The Quarán, to Muhammad.

The one hundred scriptures given to Adam, Seth, Enoch, and Abraham, are termed *Sahí-fah* (a pamphlet), and the other four, *Kitáb* (a book); but all that is necessary for the Muslim to know of these books is supposed to have been retained in the Quarán.

Luqmán-i-Hakím (supposed to have been Æsop) and Alexander the Great are also considered by Muhammadan commentators to have been prophets. Luqmán is mentioned in the thirty-first Sura of the Quarán, and Zulqurnain, "the two-horned" (supposed to have been Alexander), in the eighteenth Sura; but it is not clear as to what position the author of the Qurán intended to assign to these worthies.

Reference

1. Dr. Pfander, in the second chapter of Mizán-ul-Haqq, states that Muhammadan Doctors assert that by the descent of the *Psalms* the Torah was abrogated. Such, however, is *not* the case, for the Psalms are not said to have abrogated the Torah, and consequently David has no special title or *Kalima*.

13
The Day of Resurrection and Judgment, and the Signs of the Last Days

Qíámat (lit. "standing"), or the day of resurrection and judgment, is a time which all Muhammadans allow is a perfect secret and known only to God. But they say that the approach of the day of judgment will be known by twenty-five signs.[1]

1. The decay of faith among men.
2. The advancing of the meanest persons to dignity.
3. That a maid-servant shall become the mother of her mistress.
4. Tumults and seditions.
5. A war with the Turks.
6. Great distress in the world.
7. That the provinces of'Iráq and Syria shall refuse to pay tribute.
8. That the buildings of Medina shall extend to Yaháb.
9. The sun rising in the west.
10. The appearance of a remarkable Beast, called the *Dábbat-ul-arz,* which shall rise out of the earth in the temple at Mecca.

11. War with the Greeks and the taking of Constantinople by 70,000 of the posterity of Isaac.
12. The coming of *Masíh-ud-Dajjál*, or Anti-christ.
13. The coming of Jesus Christ, who will descend upon one of the minarets of the Mosque at Damascus.
14. War with the Jews.
15. The ravages made by *Yajúj* and *Majúj* (God and Magog)
16. A smoke which shall fill the whole earth.
17. An eclipse of the moon.
18. The return of the Arabians to idolatry.
19. The discovery of a heap of treasure by the retreating of the river Euphrates.
20. The demolition of the temple at Mecca.
21. The speaking of beasts and inanimate things.
22. A breaking out of a fire in Yaman.
23. The appearance of a remarkable man who shall drive men before him with his staff.
24. The coming of Imám Mahdí,[2] the director, who will come from Khorásán, his troops bearing black ensigns.
25. A mighty wind which shall sweep away the souls of all who have but a grain of faith in their hearts.

The following is a succinct account of the day of judgment, translated from a Muhammadan book:—"Then shall God bring all men back and raise them again, and restore to them their souls, and gather them together. He will then call for the books in which have been written the good and evil actions of all men. Then he will judge them in equity and weigh the balance (*mízán*) of their works, and will make retribution to every soul according to what he has done. Some shall enter Paradise through his goodness and mercy, and some shall go to hell. No *Muslim* shall remain in hell for ever, but shall enter into Paradise, after they have suffered according to their sins, for believers shall remain for ever in Paradise, and the unbelievers in hell fire."

Sírát is a bridge which all must pass over on the day of judgment. It is said to extend over the midst of hell, and to be sharper than the edge of a sword. In passing it the feet of the infidel will slip, and he will fall into hell fire; but the feet of the Muslim will be firm, and carry him safely to Paradise.

References

1. *See* Mishkat-ul-Musábih, bk. xxiii. chap. iii.
2. Imám Mahdí is said by the Shia'hs to have been their twelfth Imám, Abu Kásim; but who will come again in the last days.

14
Heaven

The Muhammadan Paradise is called *Jannat* (garden) in Arabic and *Bahisht* in Persian; the word *Firdaus*, from which we get our English word Paradise, being restricted to one region in the celestial abodes of bliss.

There are eight different terms employed in the Qurán for heaven, and although they would appear to be but different names for the same region, Muhammadan divines understand them to mean different stages of glory.

They are as follows[1]:

1. *Jannat-ul-Khuld* (Sura xxv. 16), "The garden of eternity."
2. *Dár-us-Salám* (Sura vi. 127), "The dwelling of peace."
3. *Dár-ul-Qarár* (Sura xl. 42), "The dwelling which abideth."
4. *Jannat-i-'Adan* (Sura ix. 72), "The garden of Eden."
5. *Jannat-ul-Mawá* (Sura xxxii. 19), "The garden of refuge."
6. *Jannat-un-N'aim* (Sura vi. 70), "The garden of delight."
7. *Jannat-i-'Illiyún* (Sura lxxxiii.18), "The garden of 'Illiyun."
8. *Jannat-ul-Firdaus* (Sura xviii.107), "The garden of Paradise."

These eight stages of Paradise are spoken of as "*eight doors*" in the traditions (Mishkát, bk. ii. chap. i.).

The sensual delights of Muhammad's Paradise are proverbial, and they must have exercised considerable influence upon the minds of the people to whom he made known his mission. The allusions in the Qurán are far too numerous to admit of quotation, but they will be found more particularly in Suras lxxvi., lv., lvi., xlvii.

The descriptions of the celestial regions and the enjoyments promised to "the faithful" are still more minutely given in the traditional sayings of the Prophet (Mishkát, bk. xxiii. chap. xiii).

Apologists for Islám, Carlyle for example, have suggested that the sensual delights of Muhammad's Paradise may after all be taken figuratively, even as the Song of Solomon and the Revelation of St. John. It is quite true that such is the interpretation hinted at in the Akhláq-i-Jaláli; and Mr. Lane in his "Modern Egyptians" says he met a Muslim of learning who considered them figurative; but such is not the view of any Muhammadan commentator. All Muslim theologians have given a literal interpretation of the sensual delights, and it is impossible for any candid mind to read the Qurán and Traditions and arrive to any other conclusion on the subject.

In addition to the seven divisions of celestial bliss, there are said to be seven firmaments (*asmán*).

1. Of pure virgin silver, which is Adam's residence.
2. Of pure gold, which is Enoch's and John Baptist's.
3. Of pearls, which is Joseph's.
4. Of white gold, which is Jesus'.
5. Of silver, which is Aaron's.
6. Of ruby and garnet, which is Moses'.
7. Of crystal, which is Abraham's.

References

1. These various stages of Paradise are variously given by European authors. Those in the text are from the Arabic dictionary, the Ghyás-ul-Loghat, and have been compared with the verses given from the Qurán.
2. *See* Dr. Adam Clark on 2 Cor. xii. 2.

15
Hell

Hell, or the place of torment, is called in Arabic *Jahannam*, and in Persian *Dozakh*; and is said to have seven portals or divisions,[1] which the Commentator Baghawi distributes as follows :—

1. *Jahannam*, for Muhammadans; for, according to the Qurán, all Muslims will pass through hell.[2]
2. *Lazwa*, a blazing fire for Christians (Sura lxx. 15 only).
3. *Hutama,* an intense fire for Jews (Sura civ. 4 only).
4 *S'áir* a flaming fire for Sabians (Sura iv. 11, and fourteen other places).
5. *Saqar*, a scorching heat for Magi (Suras liv. 58, and lxxiv. 43).
6. *Jahím*, a huge hot fire for idolaters (Sura ii. 113, and twenty other places).
7. *Háwía*, the bottomless pit for hypocrites (Sura, cl. 8).

The situation of hell is a matter of dispute.

References

1. Sura xv. 44. "It hath seven portals, and at each portal a separate band;" a tradition founded on the Talmud. Thus, in Sota 10, David is said to have rescued Absalom from

the seven dwellings of hell. (Rodwell).

2. Sura xix. 44, "Verily there is not one of you that shall not go down into hell. *Jahannam* is the Arabic from the Greek *γεέννα*, and it is remarkable that the word should be used for a purgatorial hell and not *ᾅδης* which, according to the Papists, denotes that state.

16
The Decrees of God

Taqdír, or the absolute decree and predestination of both good and evil, is the sixth article of the Muslim's creed. The orthodox belief is that whatever hath or shall come to pass in this world, whether it be good or bad, proceedeth entirely from the divine will, and is irrevocably fixed and recorded in the *preserved tablet* (*Lahw-ul-Mahfúz*).[1]

The following is a translation of an Arabic treatise on the subject: "Faith in the decrees of God, is that we believe in our heart and confess with our tongue that the most High God hath decreed all things so that nothing can happen in the world, whether it respects the conditions and operations of things, or good and evil, or obedience and disobedience, or faith and infidelity, or sickness and health, or riches and poverty, or life and death, that is not contained in the written tablet of the decrees of God. But God hath so decreed good works, obedience, and faith, that He ordains and wills them, and that they may be under His decree, His salutary direction, His good pleasure and command. On the contrary, God hath decreed, and does ordain and determine evil, disobedience, and infidelity; yet without His salutary direction, good pleasure and command, but being only by way of seduction, indignation, and prohibition. But whosoever shall say that God is not delighted with good faith, or that God hath not an indignation against evil and unbelief, he is certainly an infidel."

Reference

1. *Lahw-ul-Mahfúz*, occurs only once in the Qurán, namely, Sura lxxxv. 22, where it relates to the Qurán being written thereon. The Preserved Tablet on which the actions of men are written, is called *Imám-ul-Mubín*, the clear prototype, Sura xxxvi. 11.

17

The Five Foundations of Practical Religion

The five pillars, or foundations, of practice in Islám are :—

1. The recital of the Creed, or *Kalimah,*[1] —"There is no deity but God, and Muhammad is the Prophet of God."
2. *Sulát.*—The five stated periods of prayer.
3. *Roza.*—The thirty days fast of Ramazán.
4. *Zakát.*—The legal alms.
5. *Hajj.* — The pilgrimage to Mecca.

Reference

1. The enumeration of the *Creed* amongst the foundations of *practice* seems to perplex English writers, and consequently Dr. Macbride (p. 134), and other authors, omit it entirely, and reduce the foundations of practical religion to four. Our readers will observe, however, that it is the *recital* of the creed, and not the creed itself, which forms one of the five practical duties of the Muslim (*vide* next article).

18
The Recital of the Creed

The Recital of the *Kalimah*, or Creed, is the first of the five foundations, or pillars of practice, in Islám. It consists of the following sentence, which is always recited in Arabic:—

Lá-iláha-il-lal-laho Muhammad-ur-Rasúl-Ullah, "There is no deity but God, and Muhammad is the Apostle of God."[1]

When anyone is converted to Islám he is required to repeat this formula, and the following are the conditions required of every Muslim with reference to it:—

1. That it shall be repeated aloud, at least once in a life-time.
2. That the meaning of it shall be fully understood.
3. That it shall be believed in "by the heart".
4. That it shall be professed until death.
5. That it shall be recited correctly.
6. That it shall be always professed and declared without hesitation.

Something similar to this celebrated symbol of the Muhammadan creed appears to have existed in Arabia previous to the foundation of Islamism. Dr. Arnold in his work on "Islám and Christianity," quotes the following prayer from the writings of Abulfaraj, which is said to have been used by the idolatrous Arabians:— "I dedicate myself to Thy service. O God! Thou hast no companion, except Thy companion, of whom Thou art absolute Master of whatever is his."[2]

References

1. We have here translated *rasúl*, "Apostle," although it is generally rendered "Prophet," which, however, is the more correct rendering of *nabí*, a word which also occurs in the Qurán. Both *nabí* and *rasul* are translated into Persian and Hindustani by *paighambar*, which is translated into English by either Prophet, Apostle, or Messiah.
2. Circumcision (*Khatnah*) although never once enjoined in either the Qurán or Traditions, is an institution of Islám; but it is not incumbent upon adults, the recital of the creed being sufficient.

19
Prayer

Prayer (Arabic *Sulát*, Persian and Hindustani *Namáz*, Pushto *Nmuz*) is the second of the five foundations of practice in Islám. The constant round of devotion which characterizes Muhammadan nations is a very remarkable phenomenon in the system. We translate the words *Sulát* and *Namáz* by the English word *prayer*, although this "second foundation" of the religion of Muhammad is something quite distinct from that prayer which the Christian poet so well describes as the "soul's sincere desire uttered or unexpressed." It would be more correct to speak of the Muhammadan *Namáz* as a *service*; "prayer" being more correctly rendered by the Arabic *du'a*. In Islám prayer is reduced to a mechanical act, as distinct from a mental act; and in judging of the spiritual character of Muhammadanism, we must take into careful consideration the precise character of that devotional service which every Muslim is required to render to God at least *five* times a day,[1] and which, undoubtedly, exercises so great an influence upon the character of the followers of Muhammad.

It is absolutely necessary that the service should be performed in Arabic; and that the clothes and body of the worshipper should be clean, and that the praying place should be free from all impurity. It may be said either privately, or in company, or in a Mosque—although services in a Mosque are more meritorious than those elsewhere.

It is always preceded by ablution (*Wuzu*),[2] and, if said in a Mosque, by the *Azán* and *Iqámat*, terms which will be explained afterwards.

The regular form of prayer begins with the *Niyyat,* which is said standing, with the hands on either side:—

"I have purposed to offer up to God only, with a sincere heart this morning (or, as the case may be), with my face Qibla-wards, two (or, as the case may be) *rak'at* prayers *Farz* (*Sunnat*, or *Nafl*)."

Then follows the Takbír-i-Tahrímah, said with the thumbs touching the lobules of the ears and the open hands on each side of the face.

"God is Great !"

The Qíám, or standing position. The right hand placed upon the left, below the navel,[3] and the eyes looking to the ground in self-abasement. During which is said the Subhán[4]:—

"Holiness to thee, O God !"

"And praise be to thee !"

"Great is Thy name !"

"Great is Thy greatness !"

"There is no deity but Thee !"

The T'auuz[5] is then said as follows:—

"I seek refuge from God from cursed Satan."

After which the Tasmíyah is repeated:—

"In the name of God, the compassionate, the merciful."

Then follows the Fátihah, *viz.*, the first chapter of the Qurán[6]:—

"Praise be to God, Lord of all the Worlds !"

"The compassionate, the merciful !"

"King on the day of reckoning !"

"Thee only do we worship, and to Thee only do we cry for help."

"Guide Thou us in the straight path,"

"The path of those to whom Thou hast been gracious;"

"With whom Thou art not angry,"

"And who go not astray." — Amen.

After this the worshipper can repeat as many chapters of the Qurán as he may wish; he should, at least, recite one long or two short verses. The following chapter is usually recited, namely, the Surat-ul-Ikhlás, or the 112th chapter:

"Say: He is God alone :"

"God the eternal !"

"He begetteth not,"

"And is not begotten;"

"And there is none like unto Him."

The Takbír-i-Ruku', said whilst making an inclination of the head and body and placing the hands upon the knees, separating the fingers a little.

"God is great !"

The Tasbih-i-Ruku', said in the same posture.

"I extol the holiness of my Lord, the Great !"[7]

"I extol the holiness of my Lord, the Great !"

"I extol the holiness of my Lord, the Great !"

The Qiám-i-Sami Ullah or Tasmía', said with the body erect, but, unlike the former Qiám, the hands being placed on either side. The Imám says[8] aloud,

"God hears him who praises him."

The people then respond in a low voice.

"O Lord, Thou art praised."

Takbír-i-Sijdah, said as the worshipper drops on his knees.

"God is great!"

Tasbíh-i-Sijdah, recited as the worshipper puts first his nose and then his forehead to the ground.

"I extol the holiness of My Lord, the most High !"

"I extol the holiness of My Lord, the most High !"

"I extol the holiness of My Lord, the most High !"

Then raising his head and body and sinking backward upon his heels, and placing his hands upon his thighs, he says the Takbír-i-Jalsa.[9]

"God is great !"

Then, whilst prostrating as before, he says the Takbír-i-Sijdah.

"God is great !"

And then during the prostration the Tasbíh-i-Sijdah as before.

"I extol the holiness of My Lord, the most High !"

"I extol the holiness of My Lord, the most High !"

"I extol the holiness of My Lord, the most High !"

Then, if at the close of one rak'at, he repeats the Takbír standing, when it is called Takbír-i-Qiám; but at the end of two rakáts, and at the close of the prayer, he repeats it sitting, when it is called Takbír-i-Qa'úd.

"God is great !"

Here ends one rak'at or form of prayer. The next rak'at begins with the Fátihah or 1st chapter of the Qurán. At the close of every two rakáts he recites the Attahíyat, which is said whilst kneeling upon the ground. His left foot bent under him he sits upon it and places his hands upon his knees and says[11]:—

"The adorations of the tongue are for God, and also the adorations of the body, and alms-giving !"

"Peace be on thee, O Prophet, with the mercy of God and His blessing !"

"Peace be upon us and upon God's righteous servants !"

Then raising the first finger of the right hand he recites the Tashahhúd:—

"I testify that there is no deity but God[12]; and I testify that Muhammad is the servant of God, and the messenger of God !"[13]

The Darúd is said whilst in the same posture.

"O God, have mercy on Muhammad and on his descendants,[14] as Thou didst have mercy on Abraham and on his descendants. Thou art to be praised, and Thou are great. O God, bless Muhammad and his descendants, as Thou didst bless Abraham and his descendants !"

"Thou art to be praised, and Thou art great !"

Then the Du'a—

"O God our Lord, give us the blessings of this life, and also the blessings of life everlasting. Save us from the torments of fire."[15]

He then close with the Salám.

Turning the head round to the right, he says—

"The peace and mercy of God be with you."

Turning the head round to the left, he says—

"The peace and mercy of God be with you."

At the close of the whole set of prayers, that is, of Farz, Sunnat, Nafl, or Witr, the worshipper raises his hands[16] and offers up a "*Munájat*," or supplication. This usually consists of prayers selected from the Qurán or Hadís. They ought to be said in Arabic, although they are frequently offered up in the vernacular.

These daily prayers are either *Farz, Sunnat, Nafl*, or *Witr. Farz*, are those number of rak'ats, (or forms of prayer,) said to be enjoined by God. *Sunnat* those founded on the practice of Muhammad. *Nafl*, the voluntary performance of two rak'ats, or more, which may be omitted without sin. *Witr,* an odd number of rak'ats, either one, three, five or seven, said after the night prayer. These divisions of prayer are entirely distinct from each other. They each begin afresh with the *Niyyat.* The worshippers may rest for awhile between them, but not converse or worldly subjects. The Wahhábis think it correct to say the *Sunnat* prayers in their houses and only the *Farz* in the mozque.[17]

In order that our readers may be able to judge of the mechanism of this Muhammadan performance of prayer, we annex a time-table of the Muslim's common prayer showing the number of *rak'ats* or forms, from which it will be seen what is required of a pious Muhammadan. The five times of prayer are enjoined in the Qurán, the other three periods of prayer are voluntary. (*See* next page.)

In addition to the daily prayers, the following are special services for special occasions:

Sulát-ul-Juma'.—"The Friday Prayers." It consists of two rak'ats after the daily meridian prayer.

Sulát-ul-Musáfir:—"Prayers for a traveller." Two rak'ats instead of the usual number at the meridian, afternoon, and night prayers.

	No.	Time	The Names for the Time of Prayer: Arabie.	Persian.	Hindustant	Pushto.	The Number of Rak'ats Said: Sunnat which are optional	Sunnat before Farz.	Farz	Sunnat after Farz.	Nafl.	Witr
The Five Periods of Prayers	1.	From down to sunrise	Sulát-ul-Fajr.	Námáz-i-Subh.	Fajr-kí-Namáz	da-Sahá-rnmuz.	...	2	2	...	...	...
	2.	When the sun has begun to decline.	Sulát-ul-Zuhr	Namáz-i-Peshín.	Zohar-kí-Namáz.	da-Máspe-khín-nmuz	...	4	4	2	2	...
	3.	Mid-way between No. 2 and No. 4.	Sulát-ul-'Asar.	Namáz-i-Dígar.	'Asur-kí-Namáz.	da-Mázi-gar-nmuz.	4	...	4	...	...	...
	4.	A few minutes after sun-set.	Sulát-ul-Maghrib.	Namáz-i-Shám.	Maghrib-kí-Namáz.	da-Mákh-ám-nmuz.	...	...	3	2	2	....
	5.	When the night has closed in.	Sulát-ul-'Ishaa.	Namáz-i-Khuftan.	'Aysha-kí-Namáz.	da-Maz-khuftan-nmuz.	4	...	4	2	2	7
Three Periods Which are Voluntary	1	When the sun has well risen.	Sulát-ul-Ishráq.	Namáz-i-Ishráq	Ishráq-kí-Namáz.	da-Ishráq-nmuz.	...	...	...	...	8	...
	2	About 11 O'clock A.M.	Sulát-ul-Zuha.	Namáz-i-Chást.	Zoha-kí-Namáz.	da-Ghar-mí-nmuz.	...	...	...	...	8	....
	3.	After mid-night.	Sulát-ul-Tahajud.	Namáz-i-Tahajud.	Tahajud-kí-Namáz	da-Shape-nmuz.	...	...	...	...	9	....

Sulát-ul-Kharif.—"The prayers of fear." Said in time of war. They are two rak'ats recited first by one regiment or company and then by the other.

Sulát-ul-Táráwih.—Twenty rak'ats recited every evening during the Ramazán, immediately after the fifth daily prayer.

Sulát-ul-Istikhára.—Prayers for success or guidance. The person who is about to undertake any special business, performs two rak'at prayers and then goes to sleep. During his slumbers he may expect to have "*ilhám*," or inspiration, as to the undertaking for which he seeks guidance!

Sulát-ul-Khasúf.—Two rak'ats said at the time of an eclipse of the moon.

Sulát-ul-Kusúf.—Two rak'ats said at the time of an eclipse of the sun.

The *Azán*, is the summons to prayer proclaimed by the *Muazzin*, or crier, in small mosques from the door or side, but in large mosques it ought to be given from the minaret (*manárat*). The following is a translation, "God is great! God is great! God is great! God is great! I bear witness that there is no God but God! (repeated twice) I bear witness that Muhammad is the Apostle of God! (repeated twice). Come to prayers! Come to prayers! Come to salvation! Come to salvation ![18] God is great! There is no other God but God !"[19]

In the early morning the following sentence is added: "Prayers are better than sleep."

The *Iqámat* (fit. "causing to stand") is a recitation at the commencement of prayers in a congregation, after the worshippers have taken up their position. It is exactly the same as the *Azán*, with the addition of the words, "prayers are now ready."

The Iqámat of the Shafia' and the Wahhábis is just half the length of that of the Hanifis.

References

1. It is remarkable that there is but one passage in the Qurán in which the stated times of prayer are enjoined, and that it mentions only *four* and not five periods:— Surat-ur-Rum (xxx.), 17, "Glorify God when it is evening (*masa*), and at morning (*subh*),—and to Him be praise in the heavens and in the earth,—and at afternoon (*'ashi*), and at noon-tide (*zuhr*)." But all commentators are agreed that *masa* includes both sun-set and after sun-set; and, therefore, both the *Maghrib* and *'Ishaa* prayers.
2. *Wuzu* is the ablution of the face, hands, feet, &c., which is necessary before every time of prayer. *Ghusal,* or the washing of the whole body, is performed after certain legal defilements.
3. The Shafia', and the two other orthodox sects, place their hands on their breasts; as also the Wahháb's. The Shía'hs keep their hands on either side. In all the sects the women perform the Qíám with their hands on their breasts.
4. The Shía'hs omit the Subhán.
5. The T'auuz is also called the *'Aúzobillah.*
6. The recital of the Qurán is called the *Qira'at*, or reading.
7. The Shía'hs here add, "and with his praise." This is also added by the Shía'hs to the Tasbíh-i-Sijdah.
8. When the prayers are said by a person alone he recites both sentences.
9. The Shía'hs here omit the Takbír, and say instead' "I rise and sit by the power of God !"
10. The Shía'hs here recite the Takbír:—"God is great !" with the thumbs touching the lobules of the ear, and add, "I seek forgiveness from God, my Lord, and I repent before Him!"
11. The Shía'hs omit the Attahíyat.
12. The Shía'hs add, "who has no partner."
13. Every two rak'ats close with the Tashahhúd.
14. The Shía'hs merely recite:—"God have mercy on Muhammad and his descendants;" and omit the rest.
15. The Du'a is omitted by the Shía'hs, who recite the following instead:—"Peace be on thee, O Prophet, with

the mercy of God and His blessing!" "Peace be upon us, and upon God's righteous servants!"

16. The hands are raised in order to catch a blessing from heaven, and they are afterwards drawn over the face in order to transfer it to every part of the body.

17. Mr. Palgrave, in his "Central and Eastern Arabia," States that he observed that the Wahhábis were careless as to the legal ablutions. Perhaps he was not aware that the worshippers had performed the ablutions, and had said the *Sunnat* rak'ats privately before they came into the mosque.

18. The Shía'hs add, "Come to good works !"

19. The Shía'hs recite the last sentence twice.

20
Ramazan, or the Month of Fasting

The *Ramazán*[1] is the ninth month of the Muhammadan year, which is observed as a strict fast from the dawn of day to sunset of each day in the month. The excellence of this month was much extolled by Muhammad, who said that during Ramazán "the gates of Paradise are open, and the gates of hell are shut, and the devils are chained by the leg"; and that "only those who observe it will be permitted to enter by the gate of heaven called *Rayyán.*" Those who keep the fast "will be pardoned all their past venial sins."[2] In the month of Ramazán, Muhammad said, the Qurán began to be revealed from heaven.[3]

The fast does not commence until some Musalman is able to state that he has seen the new moon. If the sky be overclouded and the moon cannot be seen, the fast begins upon the completion of thirty days from the beginning of the previous month.

The Ramazán must be kept by every Musalman, except the sick, the infirm, and pregnant women, or women who are nursing their children. Young children, who have not reached the age of puberty, are exempt, and also travellers on a journey. In the case of a sick person or a traveller, the month's fast must be kept as soon as they are able to perform it. This is called *Qazá*, or expiration.

The fast is extremely rigorous and mortifying, and when the Ramazán happens to fall in the summer and the days are long, the prohibition even to drink a drop of water to slake the thirst is a very great hardship. Muhammad speaks of this religious exercise as "easy,"[4] as most probably it was when compared with the ascetic spirit of the times. Sir William Muir[5] thinks Muhammad did not foresee that, when he changed the Jewish intercalary year for the lunar year, that the fast would become a grievous burden instead of an easy one; but Muhammadan lexicographers say, the fast was established when the month occurred in the hot season (*see* note, p. 119).

During the month of Ramazán twenty additional *rak'ats*, or forms of prayer, are repeated after the night prayer. These are called *Taráwīh*.

Devout Muslims seclude themselves for some time in the Mosque during this month, and abstain from all worldly conversation and engage themselves in the reading of the Qurán. This seclusion is called *'Itiqáf*. Muhammad is said to have usually observed this custom for the last ten days of Ramazán.

The *Laylut-ul-Qadr,* or the "night of power," is said by Muhammad to be either on the twenty-first, twenty-third, or twenty-fifth, or twenty-seventh, or twenty-ninth. The exact date of this solemn night has not been discovered by any but the Prophet himself, and some of the Companions, although the learned doctors believe it to be on the twenty-seventh. Of this night Muhammad says in the Qurán (Surat-ul-Qadr):—

"Verily we have caused it (the Quran) to descend on the night of power.

"And who shall teach three what the night of power is?

"The night of power excelleth a thousand months;

"Therein descend the angels and the spirit by permission.

"Of their Lord in every matter;

"And all is peace till the breaking of the morn."

By these verses commentators[6] understand that on this night the Qurán came down entire in one volume to the lowest heaven, from whence it was revealed by Gabriel in portions as the occasion required. The excellences of this night are said to be innumerable, and it is believed that during it the whole animal and vegetable kingdom bow in humble adoration to the Almighty, and the waters of the sea become sweet in a moment of time! This night is frequently confounded[7] with the *Shab-i-Barát*; but even the Qurán itself does not appear to be quite clear on the subject, for in the *Surat-i-Dukhán* we read, "By this clear book. See on a *blessed night* have we sent it down, for we would warn mankind, on the night wherein all things are disposed in wisdom." In which it appears that the *blessed night*, or the *Laylut-ul-Mubarak*, is both the night of record and the night upon which the Qurán came down from heaven, although the one is supposed to be the twenty-seventh day of Ramazán, and the other the fifteenth of Shabán.

References

1. The word *Ramazán* is derived from *Ramz,* to burn. The month is said to have been so called either because it used (before the change of the calendar) to occur in the hot season, or because the month's fast is supposed to burn away the sins of men. (See *Ghyás-ul-Loghát.*)
2. Mishkát-ul-Musábih, bk. vii. chap. i, sect. 1.
3. Qurán, Surat-i-Baqr, verse 181.
4. *Ibid.*
5. Life of Mahomet, iii, p. 49.
6. Tafsír-i-Hoseini.
7. B Lane, in his "Egyptians," and by other writers.

21
Zakát, or Legal Alms-giving

Zakát (lit. "purification"), the legal alms, or poor rate, is the fourth of the five foundations of practice. Zakát should be given annually of five descriptions of property, provided they have been in possession a whole year; namely, money, cattle, grain, fruit, and merchandise. There are several minor differences amongst the various sects as to the precise explanation of the law with reference to these legal alms; but the following are the general rules observed by Sunni Musulmáns:—

1. *Money.* If he is a *Sáhib-i-Nissáb* (*i.e.* one who has had forty rupees in his possession for a year), he must give alms at the rate of one rupee in every forty, or two-and-a-half per cent.
2. *Cattle.* Should his property consist of sheep or goats, he is not obliged to give alms until they amount to forty in number. He must then give one for one hundred and twenty, and two for the next eighty, and then one for every hundred afterwards. For camels the following is the rate:—from 5 to 24, one sheep or goat; from 25 to 35, one yearling female (*bint-i-mukház*) camel; from 36 to 45, one two-year old female (*bint-i-labún*) camel; from 46 to 60, one three-year old female (*hiqqah*) camel; from 61 to 75, one four-

year old female (*jaz'ah)* camel; from 76 to 90, two two-year old female camels; from 91 to 120, two three-year old female camels; and from 121 and upwards, either a two-year old female camel for every forty, or a three-year old female camel for every fifty.

For cows or bulls:—If 30 cows, a one-year old female calf; if 40, a two-year old female calf, and so on, a one-year old female calf for every 10.

Alms for buffaloes are the same as for sheep.

For horses, either the same rate as for camels, or two rupees eight annas for every horse whose value exceeds one hundred rupees. Animals used for riding, and beasts of burden, are exempt.

3. *Fruits.* For fruits watered by rain a tenth is given; but if irrigated, then a twentieth part.

4. *Grain.* The same rates as for fruits.

5. *Merchandise.* For the capital, as well as for the profits, *Zakát* is given at the rate of one in forty, provided the owner be a Sáhib-i-nissáb. For gold bullion, half a *misqál* (= 67½ grains) is given for every 20 misqál weight. For silver bullion at the rate of 2½ per cent. For whatever is found in mines, if over 240 dirhams in weight (= 2lbs. 2 oz. 2 dr.), a fifth is required; and if the money be laid out in merchandise, alms are to be given on the profits.

   Wood and pearls are exempt, and also clothing; but not jewels.

The following are the classes of persons on whom it is lawful to bestow the Zakát:—

1. Such pilgrims to Mecca as have not the means of defraying the expenses of the journey.

2. Religious mendicants.
3. Debtors who cannot discharge their debts.
4. Beggars.
5. Poor travellers.
6. Proselytes to Muhammadanism.

The *Zakát*, or legal alms, must be distinguished from the *Sadaqa*, or offerings, which is a term more especially applied to the offerings on the *'Id-ul-Fitr* (*q.v.*) although it is used for almsgiving in general.

22

Hajj, or Pilgrimage to Mecca[1]

Hajj, or Pilgrimage to Mecca, is the fifth of the five foundations of practice. It is said, by Muhammad, to be of Divine institution, and has the authority of the Qurán for its observance.[2] Its performance is incumbent upon those men and women who have sufficient means to meet the expenses of the journey, and to maintain their families at home during their absence.

The merits of the pilgrimage are so great, that every step taken in the direction of the *K'aba* blots out a sin; and he who dies on his way to Mecca is enrolled on the list of martyrs.

The following is the orthodox way of performing the pilgrimage, founded upon the example of the "Prophet" himself.

Upon the pilgrim's, arrival at the last stage[3] near Mecca, he bathes himself, and performs two rak'at prayers, and then divesting himself of his clothes, he assumes the pilgrim's sacred robe, which is called *Ihrám*. This garment consists of two seamless wrappers, one being wrapped round the waist, and the other thrown loosely over the shoulder, the head being left uncovered. Sandals may also be worn, but not shoes or boots. After he has assumed the pilgrim's garb, he must not anoint his head, shave any part of his body, pare his nails, nor wear any other garment than the *Ihrám.* Immediately on his arrival at Mecca he performs the legal ablutions, and proceeds to the *Musjid-ul-Harám*, or Sacred Mosque, and kisses the *Hajr-ul-aswad*, or the black stone, and then encompasses the *K'aba*[4] seven times. This act, which is called *Tawáf,* is performed by commencing on the right and leaving the *K'aba* on the left. The circuits are made thrice with a quick step or run, and four times at a slow pace.[5] He then proceeds to the *Maqám-i-Ibrahím* (the place of the prophet Abraham) and performs two *rak'at* prayers, after which he turns to the black stone and kisses it. He then goes to the gate of the temple leading to Mount Safá, and from it ascends the hill and runs from the summit or Mount Safá to that of Mount Marwah seven times! On the top of the hill he remains for a few moments, and raising his hand heavenwards supplicates the Almighty.

On the eighth day, which is called *Tarwíah* he unites with his fellow-pilgrims at Miná in the usual services of the Muslim ritual, and stays the night.

After morning prayer he rushes to Mount 'Arifát, where, having said two rak'at prayers with the Imám and heard the *Khútbah* (or oration), he remains until sunset. He then proceeds to Muzdalífah, and having said the sunset and night prayers, he stays the night at that place.

The next morning, which is the *'Id-ul-Azhá*, or great feast, he comes to three places in Miná, marked by three pillars called *Jamra.* At each of these pillars he picks up seven small stones, or pebbles, and having said some particular prayer over each pebble and blown upon it, he throws it at one of the pillars. This ceremony is called *Rami-ul-Jamár*, or the throwing of pebbles.

He then proceeds to the place of sacrifice at Miná, and performs the usual sacrifice of the 'Id-ul-Azhá; after this sacrifice he gets himself shaved and his nails pared. The pilgrim garb is then removed and the pilgrimage is ended, although he should rest at Mecca the three following days, which are called the *Ayyám-ut-Tashríq*, or the days of drying up the blood of the sacrifice. These are three days of well-earned rest after the vigorous peripatetic performances of the last four days.

The pilgrimage must be performed on three days of the month of *Zul Hijja*, namely from the seventh to the tenth; a visit to Mecca at any other time has not the merit of a pilgrimage.

Before he leaves Mecca the pilgrim should once more perform the circuits round the *K'aba*, and throw stones at the sacred pillars, each seven times.

He then proceeds to Medina, and makes his salutations at the Shrine of Muhammad. The Wahhábis do not perform the last act, as it is contrary to their principles to visit shrines.

The Musulmán who has performed the pilgrimage is called *Hájí*.

The *K'aba* is also called the *Qibla*, or the direction to which Muslims are to pray. Mosques are, therefore, always erected Qiblawards.

The pilgrimage cannot be performed by proxy, as some English authors have stated, although it is considered a meritorious act to pay the expenses of one who cannot afford to perform it. But if a Muhammadan on his death-bed bequeathed a sum of money to be paid to a certain person to perform the pilgrimage, it is considered to satisfy the claims of the Muslim law. If a Muslim have the means of performing the pilgrimage, and omit to do so, its omission is equal to a *kabíra*, or mortal sin.

References

1. Only three Englishmen are known to have visited Mecca, and to have witnessed the ceremonies of the Pilgrimage — Joseph Pitts, of Exeter, A.D. 1678; John Lewis Burckhardt, A.D. 1814; Lieut. Richard Burton, of the Bombay Army, A.D. 1853. The narratives of each of these pilgrims" have been published. The first account in English of the visit of a European to Mecca, is that of Lodovico Bartema, a gentleman of Rome, who visited Mecca in 1503. His narrative was published in Willes and Eden's Decades, A.D. 1555.
2. *Vide* Qurán, Sura xxii. 28.
3. These are six in number, and are situated about five or six miles from Mecca in different directions. They are called *Míqát.*
4. Some confusion exists in the minds of English authors with regard to the word *K'aba*. The Temple or Mosque at Mecca is called Musjid-ul-Harám (the sacred Mosque), or Bait-ullah (the house of God). The *K'aba* (lit. a cube) is the square stone building in the centre, containing the black stone. And the Hajr-ul-aswad is the black stone itself, which Muslims say was originally white, but became black by reason of men's sins.
5. Sharastani informs us, that there was an opinion prevalent amongst the Arabs that the walking round the K'aba, and other ceremonies, were symbolic of the motion of the planets, and of other astronomical facts. (*Rodwell*).

23
The Law

Muhammadan law consists of two divisions, *Rawá* and *Nárawá*, *i.e.*, Things lawful and Things unlawful.

I.—That which is lawful is divided into five classes:

1. *Farz.*—That which has been enjoined in the Qurán.
2. *Wájib.*—That of which there is some doubt as to its Divine institution.
3. *Sunnat.*—The example of Muhammad, which consists of three kinds:—

   Sunnat-i-F'ilí.—That which Muhammad himself did.

   Sunnat-i-Qaulí.—That which Muhammad said should be practised.

   Sunnat-i-Taqrírí.—That which was done in the presence of Muhammad and which he did not forbid.
4. *Mustahab.*—That which Muhammad sometimes did and sometimes omitted.
5. *Mubáh.*—That which may be left unperformed without any fear of Divine punishment.

II.—Things unlawful are of three classes:—

1. *Harám.*—That which is distinctly forbidden in the Qurán and Hadís.

2. *Makrúh.*—That of which there is some doubt as to its unlawfulness, but which is generally held to be unclean or unlawful.

3. *Mufsid.*—That which is corrupting and pernicious.

The divisions of lawful and unlawful *do not merely apply to food,* but also to ablutions and other customs and precepts.

24
Sin

The Muhammadan doctors divide sins into two classes, very much as the Roman Catholic divines do; the usual Roman designation being that of *mortal* and *venial sin,* whilst Muhammadans use the expressions *Kabíra* and *Saghíra*, "Great" and "Little". *Kabíra* are those great sins, of which, if a Musalman do not repent, he will go to the purgatorial hell reserved for sinful Muslims. The divines of Islám are not agreed amongst themselves as to the exact number of Kabíra sins, but they are generally considered to be seventeen (*vide* Fawáid-us-Shari'at).

1. *Kufr*, or infidelity.
2. Constantly committing *Saghíra*, or little sins.
3. Despairing of the mercy of God.
4. Considering one's self safe from the wrath of God.
5. False witness.
6. *Qazaf*, or falsely charging a Musulman with adultery.
7. Taking a false oath.
8. Magic.
9. Drinking wine.
10. Appropriation of the property of orphans.
11. Usury.

12. Adultery.
13. Unnatural crimes.
14. Theft.
15. Murder.
16. Fleeing in battle before the face of an infidel.
17. Disobedience to parents.

25
Punishment

Punishment is divided into three classes:—

Hadd, T'azír, and *Qisás*.

1. *Hadd* is that punishment which is said to have been ordained of God in the Qurán and the Hadís, and which must be inflicted. The following belong to this class:—*Adultery*, for which the adulterer is stoned. *Fornication,* for which one hundred stripes are inflicted. *Drunkenness*, for which there are eighty stripes. The *slander of a married person,* that is, bringing a false charge of adultery against a married person, for which the offender must receive eighty lashes. This punishment is said to have been instituted by God, when 'Ayesha, the favourite wife of "the Prophet," was falsely charged with adultery! *Apostacy*, for which the *Murtadd*, or Apostate, is killed, unless he repent of his error within three days. When an Apostate from Islám has been killed according to the law, or has left the country, his property goes to those of his heirs who still remain *Musulmáns* (*vide* the "Al Sira-Jiyah").

2. *T'azír* is that punishment which is said to have been ordained of God, but of which there are not special injunctions, the exact punishment being left to the discretion of the Qází, or Judge.

3. *Qisás* (lit. "retaliation") is that punishment which can be remitted by the person offended against, upon the payment of a fine or compensation. The punishment for murder is of this class. The next akin to the murdered person can either take the life of his kinsman's murderer, or accept a money compensation (*Díat*). There is also retaliation in case of wounds. Qisás is the *lex talionis* of Moses, "eye for eye, tooth for tooth, hand for hand, foot for foot, burning for burning, wound for wound, stripe for stripe" (*vide* Exodus xxi. 24). But in allowing a money compensation for murder, Muhammad departed from the Jewish code.

26
Lawful Food

No animal is lawful food unless it be slaughtered according to the Muhammadan law, namely, by drawing the knife across the throat and cutting the windpipe, the carotid arteries, and the gullet, repeating at the same time the words "*Bismillah Allaho Akbar,*" *i.e.* "In the name of the great God." A *clean* animal, so slaughtered, becomes lawful food.

In the "Sharah Waqaia" it is said that the following creatures are lawful (*halál*):—

1. Those animals that are cloven-footed and chew the cud, and are not beasts of prey.
2. Birds that do *not* seize their prey with their claws, or wound them with their bills, but pick up food with their bills.
3. Fish; but no other animals which move in the water.
4. Locusts.

Some commentators say that the horse is lawful; but it is generally held to be "*makrúh*".

Fish found dead in the water is unlawful; but if it be taken out and die afterwards it is lawful.

Alligators, turtles, crabs, snakes, frogs, etc., are unlawful. Wine is expressly forbidden in the Qurán; and, in the judgement of the learned, this prohibition extends to whatever has a tendency to intoxicate, such as opium, bhang, chars,[1] and tobacco. The Akhund of Swat[2] his issued several "*fatwáns,*" prohibiting the use of tobacco; but the chilam (or pipe), having become a national institution, no notice has been taken of the inhibition. The Wahhábis do not permit territory, the hukka, or chilam, is never allowed in a mosque.

References

1. Bhang and Chars are intoxicating preparations of hemp.
2. The Akhund is Swát is a great religious leader amongst the Muhammadans of North India and Central Asia. He resides at Seydú, in Swát, about twenty miles beyond the British frontier.

27
Farz-i-Kafáí

Farz-i-Kafáí are those commands which are imperative (*farz*); but which, if one person in eight or ten perform, it is equivalent to all having performed it.

1. To return a salutation.
2. To visit the sick, and inquire after their welfare.
3. To follow a bier on foot to the grave.
4. To accept an invitation.
5. To reply to a sneeze, *e.g.* if a person sneeze, and say immediately afterwards, "God be praised" (*Alhamdo lillah)*, it is incumbent upon at least one of the party to exclaim, "God have mercy on you" (*Yarhamuk Allah*).

There is an interesting chapter on the custom of saluting after sneezing in Isaac D'Israeli's "Curiosities of Literature," from which it appears that it is almost universal amongst nations.

28
Fitrat

Fitrat (lit. "nature") is said to be certain ancient practices of the prophets before the time of Muhammad, which have not been forbidden by him.

In the Hadís "*Muslim,*" the customs of *fitrat* are said to be ten in number.

1. The clipping of the mustachios, so that they do not enter the mouth.
2. Not cutting or shaving the beard.
3. Cleaning the teeth (*i.e., miswák*).
4. Cleansing the nostrils with water at the usual ablutions.
5. Cutting the nails.
6. Cleaning the finger-joints.
7. Pulling out the hairs under the arms.
8. *   *   *   *
9. *   *   *   *
10. Cleansing the mouth with water at the time of ablution.

29
Salutations

The usual Muhammadan salutation is "*as salámu 'alekam,*" *i.e.* "The peace of God be with you."

When a person makes a "*salám,*" and any of the assembly rise and return it, it is considered sufficient for the whole company.

The lesser number should always be the first to salute the greater; he who rides should salute him who walks; he who walks, him who stands; the stander, the sitter, etc. A man should not salute a woman on the road; and it is considered very disrespectful to salute with the left hand, that hand being used for legal ablutions.

The ordinary salute is made by raising the right hand either to the breast or to the fore-head.

In Central Asia the salutation is generally given without any motion of the hand or body.

Pupils salute their masters by kissing the hand or sleeve, which is the usual salutation made to men of eminent piety.

Homage is paid by kissing the feet of the ruler, or by kissing the ground or carpet.

In Afghanistan, conquered people pay homage by casting their turbans at the feel of the conqueror; and the heads of tribes often lessen the size of their turbans before appearing in the presence of their rulers.

30
The Caliph

The Caliph, or *Khalífa* (*i.e.,* the *vicegerent* of the Prophet), is the sovereign dignity amongst Muhammadans, vested with absolute power. The word more frequently used for the office in Muhammadan works of jurisprudence is *Imám* (leader), or *Imám-ul-'Azam* (the great leader). It is held to be an essential principle in the establishment of the office, that there shall be only one Caliph at the same time; for the Prophet said: — "When two Caliphs have been set up, put the last to death and preserve the second, for the last is a rebel" (*vide* Mishkát, bk. xvi. chap. i.) According to all Sunní Muhammadan books, it is absolutely necessary that the Caliph be "a man, an adult, a sane person, a free man, a learned divine, a powerful ruler, a just person, and one of the Quraish" (*i.e. of* the tribe to which the Prophet himself belonged). The Shía'hs, of course, hold that he should be one of the descendants of the Prophet's own family; but this is rejected by the Sunnis and Wahhábis. The condition that the Caliph should be of the Quraish, is very important; for thereby the present Ottoman Sultans fail to establish their claims to the Caliphate.

After the deaths of the first five Caliphs, — Abn Bakr, Omar, Osmán, Ali, and Hasan,—the Caliphate, which is allowed by all parties to be *elective*, and not hereditary, passed successively to the Ommiades and Abbasides. The temporal power of the Abbaside Caliphs was overthrown by Houlakon Khan, son of the celebrated Jengiz Khán, A.D. 1258; but, for three centuries, the descendants of the Abba-side, or Bagdad, Caliphs resided in Egypt, and asserted their claim to the spiritual power.

The founder of the present dynasty of Ottoman Sultans was Osman, the son of a tribe of Oghouz Turks, a powerful chief, whose descendant, Bazazet I, is said to have obtained the title of *Sultán* from one of the Abbaside Caliphs in Egypt, A.D. 1389. When Selim I. conquered Egypt (A.D. 1516), it is asserted that he obtained a transfer of the title of Caliph to himself from one of the successors of the old Bagdad Caliphs. It is, however, a mere assertion; for the title and office being elective, and not hereditary, it was not in the power of any Caliph to transfer it to another. Force of circumstances alone has compelled the ruler of the Ottoman Empire to assume the position, and has induced his subjects to acquiesce in the usurpation. We have not seen a single work of authority, nor met with a single man of learning, who has ever attempted to prove that the Sultans of Turkey are rightful Caliphs; for the assumption of the title by any one who is not of the Quraish tribe is undoubtedly illegal and heretical, as will be seen from the following authorities :—

(*Mishkát-ul-Musábih*, bk. xxiv. chap xii.)

"Ibn-i-Umr relates that the Prophet of God said:—'The Caliphs shall be in the Quraish tribe as long as there are two persons in it, one to rule and another to serve.' "

(*Sharh-ul-Muwáqif*, p. 606. Arabic Edition. Egypt.)

"It is a condition that the Caliph (*Imám*) be of the Quraish tribe. All admit this, except the Khawárij and certain Mutazilahs. We all say with the Prophet: 'Let the Caliph be of the Quraish'; and it is certain that the Companions acted upon this injunction, for Abu Bakr urged it as an authority upon the Ansárs, on the day of Sakhifah, when the Companions were present and agreed.

It is, therefore, for a certainty established that the Caliph must be of the Quraish."

(The *Hujjat-Ullah-al-Bálaghah*, p. 335. Arabic Edition, Delhi.)

"It is a necessary condition that the Caliph (*Imám*) be of the Quraish tribe."

(The *Kashháf-i-Istaláhat*. A Dictionary of Technical Terms. Edited by Colonel N. Lees, *in loco*.)

"The Caliph (*Imám*) must be a Quraish."

31
Muhammadan Clergy, Scholars, and Saints

The Muslims have no hereditary priestly caste as the Hindus, nor have they a distinct order of clergy exactly corresponding with those of the Christian Church. But still there is a powerful hierarchy possessed of great political and religious influence.

In countries under Muhammadan rule the religious dignitaries are appointed by the king, who is properly the highest spiritual authority in the kingdom. The Shekh·ul-Islám at Constantinople unites in himself the functions of the Primate and Lord Chancellor.

The following are the chief religious functionaries, in a state governed according to Muhammadan law.

Qázi'.—The minister of justice, who passes sentence in all cases of law; religious, moral civil, or criminal.

Mufti'.—The law officer who expounds the law, and in difficult cases supplies the *Qázi'* with "*fatwas*" or decisions.

There are still persons in India bearing the titles of *Qázi'* and *Mufti'*, but the offices have ceased to exist under British Government. The Indian law, however, permits *civil* cases being decided by Muhammadan divines, if both parties consent to the arrangement.

Imám.—The Arabic word *Imám* is said, by Sale, to

answer to the Latin *antistes*, the president of the temple. It is also used for the four successors of Muhammad, the four great doctors of the four orthodox sects, the twelve great leaders of the Shía'hs, and for any great religious leader. It is, however, commonly used for the person who leads the daily prayer, and is in receipt of the revenues of the mosque.

The titles of *Qázi*́, *Mufti*́, and *Imám* may be said to embrace the various appointments held by Muhammadan divines; but there are also numerous titles to denote doctors of Science and Divinity.

Tabib. A doctor of medicine.

Hakím. A doctor of philosophy, used also for a doctor of medicine.

Muhaqqiq. A very learned doctor in one or two sciences.

Maulawí, also *Mullá*. A doctor of divinity used for any person who has been educated in the Muhammadan religion, and assumes the office of teacher.

Faqih. A doctor of law.

Mutakallim. A doctor of theology.

Muhaddis. A doctor of the law of the traditions.

Mufassir. One learned in the commentaries on the Qurán.

Madarrís. An academical doctor, *i.e.*, one educated in some school of reputation.

Doctors of Divinity are of three grades: *Maulaví*, *'Alim* (pl. *'Ulama*), *Mujtahid* (pl. *Mujtahidín*). The title of *Mujtahid* is held by very few Sunní Muhammadans, but is more common amongst the Shía'hs.

In addition to these titles, which express the degree of learning, there are others which denote the piety and sanctity of the individual. *Pír* and *Walí* are the common titles; but the following express certain degrees of reputed sanctity :—

'A'bid, one constantly engaged in the worship of God.

Záhid, one who leads a life of asceticism. The title of *Faqír* does not always denote one who has renounced the possessions of the world, but is applied to any one of a humble spirit, one poor in the sight of God, rather than in need of worldly assistance.

Qutbah and *Ghaus*, the highest orders of sanctity. According to vulgar tradition, a Ghaus is a saint whose ardour of devotion, is such, that in the act of worship his head and limbs fall asunder! whilst a *Qutbah* is one who is supposed to have attained to the state of sanctity which reflects the heart of the Prophet.

There are four titles of respect which scarcely belong to either the religious or the learned classes, but are of more general use:—

Shekh, an appellation which literally signifies an elder or aged person. It is a common title of respect, and is almost synonymous with our English "*Mister*". In Egypt and Arabia it appears to be used for the Hindustani and Persian *Khán*, or chief.

Miyán, (lit. "a master" or "friend") generally used for the descendants of celebrated saints, but also as a title of respect.

Sayyid, generally pronounced *Syud* (lit. "lord"). For the descendants of Muhammad from the daughter Fatimah and her husband 'Ali. The word Sayyid is often used as part of a name, without reference to family descent from the Prophet; as Sayyid Ahmad, Sayyid Shah, & c.

Mír, also used for Sayyids, but not exclusively.

32
Theological Literature

Muhammadan theological literature is very extensive, and in consequence of the cheapness of lithographic printing, it is daily increasing.

The following are its chief divisions :—

1. *Hadís*.—Accounts of the precepts and practice of Muhammad. The collectors of Hadís may be numbered by hundreds, but the chief authorities are the six books known as the *Siháh-i-Sita*, or "*six correct books*". The popular work on the subject amongst the Sunnis of India being the Mishkát-ul-Musábih. (*See* article on Traditions.)
2. *Usúl* (lit. "roots").—Treatises on the rules and principles of the four foundations of the Islám law, — being expositions of the exegesis of the Qurán and Hadís, and the principles of Ijma' and Qiás. The most popular works on this subject are the Manár, by Abdullah ibn Ahmad, A.H. 710, and the *Talwi' Tauzia*,' by 'Ubaid-Ullah ibn Mas'ud, A.H. 747.
3. *'Aqáid* (lit. "creeds").—Expositions of scholastic theology, founded upon the six articles of faith. The most celebrated exposition of the Islám creed being that by Imám Ghazáli, A.H. 505. In India the work most read is the *Sharah-i-Aqáid,* by Maulaví Mas'ud S'ad-ud-din Taftazáni, A.H. 792.

4. *Fiqah.*—Works on Muhammadan law, whether civil or religious. The work most read amongst Sunnis is the *Hidáyah*, written by a learned man named 'Ali, A.H. 593; part of which has been translated by the late Colonel Charles Hamilton. A smallar work, entitled the *Sharah Waqaiah,* by Abdul Haqq, is also much used.

5. *Tajsír.*—Commentaries on the Qurán. These are very numerous, and contain very many Jewish traditions of the most worthless character. One of the latest and most learned of these productions is said to be the short commentary by Shah Wali Ullah of Delhi, who died A.H. 1176.

   The best known commentaries amongst the Sunnis are Baizáwi (A.H. 685), Madárik (A.H. 701), Jalálain (A.H. 911), Baghawi (A.H. 515), Mazhári (A.H. 1225), *Hoseini* (A.H. 900).

6. *Síyar.*—Ecclesiastical history, *i.e.*, the history of Muhammad and his successors. This branch of literature, Sayyid Ahmad Khan of Aligarh says, "is the one which requires the most emendation."

The chief authorities on the life of Muhammad and early days of Islám, in addition to the Hadís, are Ibn Isháq, Ibn Hishám, Wáqidi, and Tabarí; whilst the most popular histories amongst the Sunnis of India are the Rawzat-ul-Ahbáb, by 'Ataa Ullah ibn Fazl Ullah, A.H. 1000, and the Madárij-un-Nabuwat, by Shekh Abdul Haqq, A.H. 1025.

In addition to his theological studies, the Muhammadan student is instructed in *Mantiq* (logic), *Sarf* (inflexion), and *Nahw* (syntax).

The text of a book is called *Matan*, the marginal notes *Hashíyah*, and its commentary *Sharh.*

33
Muharram and 'Áshuráa

The *Muharram* (lit. "that which is sacred") commences on the first of the month[1] of that name, and is continued for ten days, the tenth day being called *'Ashuráa*. They are days of *matam*, or lamentation, in commemoration of the martyrdom of 'Ali, and of Hasan, and Husain,[2] as observed by the Shía'hs; but the day 'Áshuraa (the tenth) is also held sacred by the Sunnís, the observance of the month having been enjoined by Muhammad on account of its having been the month of creation.

The ceremonies of the Muharram differ much in different places; but the following are the main features of the festival as observed by the Shía'hs. A place is prepared which is called the *'Áshúr-khána* (the ten-day house), or *Imám-Bára* (the Imám place), in the centre of which is dug a pit, in which fires are kindled, and at night the people, young and old, fence across the fire with sticks and swords, and whilst dancing round it, call out, "Oh 'Ali! noble Hasan! noble Husain! bridegroom! alas friend! stay! stay!" etc.; the cry being repeated in the most excited manner hundreds of times, until the whole assembly has reached the highest pitch of excitement. They then form themselves in circles, and beat themselves with chains in the most frantic manner. The women repeat a funeral eulogium, and the Maulavís, the *Rowzat-us-Shuhádáa*, or the Book of Martyrs.

On the seventh day there are representations of the marriage ceremony of Qásim, and of the martyrdom of Husain; and on the eighth day a lance or spear is carried about the city to represent Husain's head, which was carried on the point of a javelin by order of Yazíd. In addition to these representations, there are the Tázías, Tábúts, or biers, of the tombs of Hasan and Husain, a horse-shoe in representation of Husain's swift horse, and the standards of Hasan, Husain, and Qásim, and other Muslim celebrities.

The Sunní Muhammadans do not usually take part in these ceremonies, but observe the tenth day, *'Ashuráa*, being the day on which God is said to have created Adam and Eve, heaven, hell, the tablet of decree, the pen, fate, life, and death.

Muhammad commanded his followers to observe the *'Áshuráa* by bathing, wearing new clothes applying *Surma*[3] to the eyes, fasting, prayers, making peace with one's enemies, associating with religious persons, relieving orphans, and giving of alms.

The fast of *'Áshuráa* is a *Sunnat fast, i.e., not* founded upon an injunction in the Qurán, but upon the example of Muhammad.

References

1. The twelve months of the Muhammad lunar year are as follows:—

1.	Muharram	The sacred month.
2.	Safar	The month which is void.
3.	Rabi'-ul-awwal	The first of spring.
4.	Rabi'-ul-ákhir	The last of spring.
5.	Jamád-al-úlá	The first dry month.
6.	Jamád-al-ukhrá	The last of spring.
7.	Rajab.	The revered month.

8. Sh'abán	The month of division
9. Ramazán	The hot month.
10. Shawwál	The month for going forth (hunting).
11. Zul-Q'ada	The month of rest.
12. Zul-Hijja	The month of pilgrimage.

2. The Khalífa 'Ali was assassinated in the Mosque of Cufa, A.D. 660. Hasan was poisoned by his wife, at the instigation of Yazíd. Husain was slain, with three and thirty strokes of lances and swords, A.D. 680. The story of Husain is one of the most touching pages of Muslim history.

3. Surma is antimony or galena ground to a fine powder; and applied to the eyelids to improve the brightness of the eyes.

34
Ákhiri Chahár Shamba

Ákhiri Chahár Shamba is the "*last Wednesday*" of the month of Safar, and is a feast held in commemoration of Muhammad's having experienced some mitigation of his last illness and having bathed. It was the last time he performed the legal bathing, for he died on the twelfth day of the next month. In some parts of Islám it is customary, in the early morning of this day, to write seven verses of the Qurán, known as the *Seven Salâms*, and then wash off the ink and drink it as a charm against evil.

The Ákhiri Chahár Shamba is not observed by the Wahhábís, not being enjoined in the Qurán and Hadís.

Reference

1. The Persian name for the day; the Arabic being *Arb'áa-ul-Akhír, i.e.* "the last Wednesday."

35
Bára Wafát[1]

The *Bára Wafat* (*i.e., Bára*, "twelve," and *Wafát*, "death") is the twelfth day of the month, Rabí-ul-Awwal. It is observed in commemoration of Muhammad's death.

On this day, *Fátihahs* (*i.e.,* the first chapter of the Qurán), are said for Muhammad; and both in private houses and in the mosques, the learned recite portions of the Traditions and other works in praise of the excellences of Muhammad. These customs are usually observed for the whole twelve days, although the twelfth day is held most sacred.

The Wahhábís do not observe the *Bára Wafát*, as its observance is not enjoined in the Qurán or Hadís.

Reference

1. The Hindustani name of the day, there being no special title for the day in Persian or Arabic.

36
Shab-i-Bará't[1]

Shab-i-Barát, the "night of record," is observed on the fifteenth day of the month, Sh'abán. It is the "Guy Fawkes Day" of India, being the night for display of fireworks.

On this night, Muhammad said, God registers annually all the actions of mankind which they are to perform during the year; and that all the children of men, who are to be born and to die in the year, are recorded. Muhammad enjoined his followers to keep awake the whole night, to repeat one hundred *rak'at* prayers, and to fast the next day; but there are generally great rejoicings instead of a fast, and large sums of money are spent in fireworks. The Shab-i-Barát must not be confounded with the *Laylat-ul-Qadr* (night of power), mentioned in the Qurán, which is the twenty-seventh night of the Ramazán. The *Shab-i-Barát,* however, is frequently called *Shab Qadr*, or the night of power, by the common people.

Reference

1. The Persian title; the Arabic being *Laylat-ul-Mubaraka.*

37
’Id-ul-Fitr, or the Lesser Festival

‘Id-ul-Fitr (lit. “the feast of breaking the fast”), is called also the feast of Ramazán, the Feast of Alms, and the Minor Festival. It is held on the first day of the month of Shawwál, which is the day after the close of the Ramazán fast. On this day, before going to the place of prayer, the *Sadaqa*, or propitiatory offerings, are made to the poor in the name of God. The offerings having been made, the people assemble either in the Jama’-i-Masjid (*i.e.*, the principal mosque), or proceed to the *’Idgah*, which is a special place of worship on festivals. The worship commences with two *rak’at* prayers, after which the Imám takes his place on the second step of the *mimbar* (pulpit) and recites the *Khutbah,* concluding with a prayer for the king. After this is ended, he offers up a *munáját*, or supplication, for the people, for the remission of sins, the recovery of the sick, increase of rain, abundance of corn, preservation from misfortune, and freedom from debt. He then descends to the ground, and makes further supplication for the people, the congregation saying *Amín* at the end of each supplication. At the close of the service the members of the congregation salute and embrace each other, and offer mutual congratulations, and then return to their homes, and spend the rest of the day in feasting and merriment.

38
’Id-ul-Azhá, or the Feast of Sacrifice

Id-ul-Azhá,[1] or the Feast Or Sacrifice is called also *Yaum-un-Nahr, Qurbán-i-’Id, Qurbán Bayrám, Baqr-i-’Id* (the Cow Festival) and the Great Feast, and is held on the tenth day of the month Zul-Hijja. This festival has become part of the Meccan pilgrimage, of which it is the concluding scene, although it appears that Muhammad at first intended to conform to the custom of the Jews in observing the great day of atonement, but when he failed to maintain a friendly footing with the Jews, he merged the rite into the Meccan pilgrimage. This feast, however, is the great Muhammadan festival, which is observed wherever Islám exists; and it is a notable fact that whilst Muhammad professed to abrogate the Jewish ritual, and also ignored entirely the doctrine of the atonement as taught in the New Testament, denying even the very fact of our Saviour’s crucifixion, he made the “*day of sacrifice*”. the great central festival of his religion.

There is a very remarkable Hadís, related by ’Áyesha, who states that Muhammad said, “Man hath not done anything on the ’Id-ul-Azhá more pleasing to God than spilling blood; for verily the animal sacrificed will come, on the day or resurrection, with its horns, its hair, and its hoofs, and will make the scales of his (good) actions heavy.

Verily its blood reacheth the acceptance of God, before it falleth upon the ground, therefore, be joyful in it."[2] The animal sacrificed must be without blemish, and of full age; but it may be either a goat, a sheep, a cow, or a camél.

According to the commentator Jalál-ud-dín Syúty, the sacrifice was instituted in commemoration of Abraham's willingness to sacrifice his son *Ismaíl*! The following is the account given by Muhammadan writers:—"When Ibrahim (the peace of God be upon him) founded Mecca, the Lord desired him to prepare a feast for him. Upon Ibrahím's (the friend of God) requesting to know what. He would have on the occasion, the Lord replied, 'Offer up thy son Ismaíl.' Agreeably to God's command he took Ismaíl to the K'aba to sacrifice him, and having laid him down, he made several ineffectual strokes on his throat with a knife, on which Ismaíl observed, 'Your eyes being uncovered, it is through pity and compassion for me you allow the knife to miss: it would be better if you blindfolded yourself with the end of your turban and then sacrificed me.' Ibrahím acted upon his son's suggestion and having repeated the words '*bismillah allah ho akbar*' (*i.e.*, 'in the name of the great God') he drew the knife across his son's neck. In the meanwhile, however, Gabriel had substituted a broad-tailed sheep for the youth Ismaíl, and Ibrahím unfolding his eye observed, to his surprise, the sheep slain, and his son standing behind him." The account is a ridiculous parody upon the words of the inspired prophet Moses. In the Qurán the name of the son is not given, although commentators state, that the Prophet said that he was a descendant of the son of Abraham who was offered in Sacrifice.[3] The sacrifice, as it is now performed on the 'Id-ul-Azhá, is as follows:— The people assemble for prayer at the 'Idgah as on the 'Id-ul-Fitr; after prayers the people return to their houses. The head of the family then takes a sheep (or a cow or camel) to the entrance of his house and sacrifices it, by repeating the words, "In the name of the great God," and cutting its throat. The flesh of the animal is then divided, two-thirds being kept by the family, and one-third being given to the poor in the name of God.

References

1. Vulg. *'Id-uz-Zohá.*
2. Mishkat-ul-Masábih, bk. iv. chap. xliii, sect. 2.
3. The name is not given in the Qurán, but it is in the Hadís Sahíh Bokhári.

39
Nikah, or Marriage

Nikah, is the celebration of the marriage contract as distinguished from the festive rejoicings which usually accompany it; the latter being called *Shádí* in Persian and Urdú, and *'Urs* in Arabic.

Marriage, according to Muhammadan law, is simply a *civil* contract, and its validity does not depend upon any religious ceremony.

The legality of marriage depends upon the consent of the parties, which is called *I'jáb* and *Qabúl*, *viz.*, declaration and acceptance; the presence of two male witnesses, or one male and two females;[1] and a dower of not less than ten dirhems to be settled upon the woman. The omission of the settlement does not, however, invalidate the contract; for, under any circumstances, the woman becomes entitled to her dower of ten dirhems or more. Muhammadans are permitted by the Qurán[2] to marry four free women, and to have as many female slaves as he may possess. Marriages for a limited period were sanctioned by "the Prophet"; but this law is said to have been abrogated, although it is allowed by the Shía'hs even in the present day. These temporary marriages are called *Mut'ah*, and are undoubtedly the greatest blot in Muhammad's moral legislation.

Marriage is enjoined upon every Muslim, and celibacy

is frequently condemned by Muhammad. The "clergy" are all married men, and even the *ascetic* orders are, as George Herbert would have said, "rather married than unmarried." It is related in the Hadís, that Muhammad said that, "when the servant of God marries, he perfects half his religion." Not long ago we met a Faqír of the Nukshbandía order, a man of considerable reputation at the court of Cabul, who said that he wished to lead a celibate life, but that his disciples had insisted upon his "perfecting his religion" by entering upon the married state!

As the religious ceremony does not form part of the legal conditions of marriage, there is no uniformity of ritual observed in its celebration. Some Qázís merely recite the *Fátihah* (the first chapter of the Qurán), and the *Darúd*, or blessing; but the following is the more common order of performing the service. The Qází, the bridegroom, and the bride's attorney, with the witnesses having assembled in some convenient place, arrangements are made as to the amount of Dower, or *Mahr.* The bridegroom then repeats after the Qází the following:—

1. The *Istighfár*, "I desire forgiveness from God, who is my Lord."
2. The four chapters of the Qurán commencing with the word "*Qul*". These chapters have nothing in them connected with the subject of marriage, and appear to be selected on account of their brevity.
3. The *Kalima*, or Creed. "There is no deity but God, and Muhammad is the Prophet of God."
4. The *Sift-ul-Imán*. A profession of belief in God, the angels, the scriptures, the prophets, the resurrection, and in fate or absolute decree of good and evil.

The Qází then requests the bride's attorney to take

the hand of the bridegroom, and to say, "Such an one's daughter, by the agency of her attorney, and by the testimony of two witnesses, has, in your marriage with her, had such a dower settled upon her, do you consent to it?" To which the bridegroom replies, "With my whole heart and soul, to my marriage with this woman as well as to the dower already settled upon her, I consent, I consent, I consent !"

After this the Qází raises his hands, and offers the following prayer:—

"O great God! grant that mutual love may reign between this couple, as it existed between Adam and Eve, Abraham and Sarah, Joseph and Zulekha,[3] Moses and Zipporah, his Highness Muhammad and 'Áyesha, and his Highness 'Ali Murtuza and Fátimah-uz-Zahra."

The ceremony being over, the bridegroom embraces his friends and receives their congratulations. Nikah is preceded and followed by festive rejoicings, which have been variously described by Oriental travellers; but they are not parts of either the civil or religious ceremony.

References

1. In Muhammadan law woman, instead of being man's "better half," is only equal to half a man!
2. "Of women who seem good in your eyes marry two, or three, or four; and if ye fear that ye shall not act equitably, then one only, or the slaves whom ye have acquired." (Sura, iv. 3.)
3. According to Muhammad, Joseph afterwards married Zulekha, the widow of Potiphar.

40
Taláq, or Divorce

In Islám the wife is the property of the husband, and consequently she can be disposed of by divorce at a moment's notice. The law has, however, placed certain slight restrictions upon the exercise of this right, and has ruled that there are three kinds of divorce:—

1. *Taláq-i-Ahsan*, or "the *most laudable* form of divorce," is when the husband divorces his wife when she is in a state of purity, by one sentence, "*thou art divorced,*" or words to that effect. This is esteemed the best form, because the sentence having been only pronounced *once*, the husband can again change his mind, with the consent of his divorced wife, at any subsequent period, until she marries another.
2. *Taláq-i-Hasan,* or "a *laudable* form of divorce," is when the husband divorces his wife by pronouncing the sentence, "*thou art divorced,*" during his wife's period of purity, and at intervals of a month.
3. *Taláq-i-Bid'aí*, or "an *irregular* form of divorce," is when the husband repeats the sentence three times on one occasion.

Whenever the sentence of divorce is repeated three times it is a *Taláq-i-Mutlaq*, or an irrevocable divorce, after which the husband cannot marry his repudiated wife until she has married and lived with another, and is divorced by her second husband.

In all cases of repudiation, except when a wife requests her husband to divorce her, the dower must be repaid to the woman, an arrangement which often prevents a man exercising the privilege.

41
Janáza, or Burial

Janáza is the term used both for the bier and for the Muhammadan funeral service. The burial service is founded upon the practice of Muhammad, and varies but little in different countries, although the ceremonies connected with the funeral procession are diversified. In Egypt, for instance, the male relations and friends of the deceased precede the corpse, whilst the female mourners follow behind. In North India and Central Asia, women do not usually attend funerals, and the friends and relatives of the deceased walk behind the bier. There is a tradition amongst some Muhammadans that no one should precede the corpse, as the angels go before. Funeral processions in Central Asia are usually very simple in their arrangements, and are said to be more in accordance with the practice of the "Prophet," than those of Egypt and Turkey. It is considered a very meritorious act to carry the bier, and four from among the near relations, every now and then relieved by an equal number, carry it on their shoulders. Unlike our Christian custom of walking slowly to the grave, Muhammadans carry their dead quickly to the place of interment; for Muhammad is related to have said, that it is good to carry the dead quickly to the grave to cause the righteous person to arrive soon at happiness, and if he be a bad man it is well to put wickedness away from one's shoulders. Funerals should always be attended on foot; for it is said, that Muhammad on one occasion rebuked his people for following a bier on horse-back. "Have you no shame?" said he, "since God's angles go on foot, and you go upon the back of quadrupeds?" It is a highly meritorious act to attend a funeral, whether it be that of a Muslim, a Jew, or a Christian.

The Muhammadan funeral service is not recited in the graveyard, it being too polluted a place for so sacred an office; but either in a mosque, or in some open space near the dwelling of the deceased person, or the graveyard. The owner of the corpse, *i.e.*, the nearest relative, is the proper person to recite the service; but it is usually said by the family Imám, or the village Qází.

The following is the order of the service:—

Some one present calls out, —

"Here begin the prayers for the dead."

Then those present arrange themselves in three, five, or seven rows opposite the corpse, with their faces Qiblawards (*i.e.,* towards Mecca). The Imám stands in front of the ranks opposite the head[1] of the corpse, if it be that of a male, or the waist, if it be that of a female.

The whole company having taken up the *Qíám*, or standing position, the Imám recites the Niyat.

"I purpose to perform prayers to God, for this dead person, consisting of four *Takbírs.*"

Then placing his hands to the lobes of his ears, he says the first *Takbír*.

"God is great !"

Then folding his hands, the right hand placed upon the left, below the navel, he recites the *Subhán* :—

"Holiness to Thee, O God,"

"And to Thee be praise."

"Great is Thy Name."

"Great is Thy Greatness."

"Great is Thy Praise."[2]

"There is no deity but Thee."

Then follows the second *Takbír* :—

"God is great !"

Then the *Darúd*:—

"O God, have mercy on Muhammad and upon his descendants, as Thou didst bestow mercy, and peace, and blessing, and compassion, and great kindness upon Abraham and upon his descendants."

"Thou art praised, and Thou art great !"

"O God, bless Muhammad and his descendants, as Thou didst bless and didst have compassion and great kindness upon Abraham and upon his descendants."

Then follows the third *Takbír* :—

"God is great !

After which the following prayer (*Dua'*) is recited:—

"O God, forgive our living and our dead, and those of us who are present, and those who are absent, and our children, and our full grown persons, our men and our women. O God, those whom Thou dost keep alive amongst us, keep alive in Islám, and those whom Thou causest to die, let them die in the Faith."

Then follows the fourth *Takbír* :—

"God is great !"

Turning the head round to the right, he says:—

"Peace and mercy be to Thee."

Turning the head round to the left, he says:—

"Peace and mercy be to Thee."

The *Takbír* is recited by the Imám aloud, but the *Subhán,* the *Salám*, the *Darúd*, and the *Dua'*, are recited by the Imám and the people in a low voice.

The people then seat themselves on the ground, and raise their hands in silent prayer in behalf of the deceased's soul, and afterwards addressing the relatives they say, "It is the decree of God." To which the chief mourner replies, "I am pleased with the will of God." He then gives permission to the people to retire by saying, "There is permission to depart."

Those who wish to return to their houses do so at this time, and the rest proceed to the grave. The corpse is then placed on its back in the grave, with the head of the north and feet to the south, the face being turned towards Mecca. The persons who place the corpse in the grave repeat the following sentence: "We commit thee to earth in the name of God and in the religion of the Prophet."

The bands of the shroud having been loosed, the recess, which is called the *láhd*, is closed in with unburnt bricks and the grave filled in with earth. In some countries it is usual to recite the *Súrat i Twá Háh* as the clods of earth are thrown into the grave; but this practice is objected to by the Wahhábís, and by many learned divines. This chapter is as follows:—

"From it (the earth) have We (God) created you, and unto it will We return you, and out of it will We bring you forth the second time."

After the burial, the people offer a *fátihah* (*i.e.*, the first chapter of the *Qurán*) in the name of the deceased, and again when they have proceeded about forty paces from the grave they offer another *fátihah*; for at this juncture, it is said, the two angles Munkar and Nakír examine the deceased as to his faith.[3] After this, food is distributed to beggars and religious mendicants as a propitiatory offering to God, in the name of the deceased person.

If the grave be for the body of a woman, it should be to the height of a man's chest, if for a man, to the height of the waist. At the bottom of the grave the recess is made on the side to receive the corpse, which is called the *láhad*. The dead are seldom interred in coffins, although they are not prohibited.

To build tombs with stones or burnt bricks, or to write a verse of the Qurán upon them, is forbidden in the Hadís; but largest one and brick tombs are common to all Muhammadan countries, and very frequently they bear inscriptions.

On the third day after the burial of the dead, it is usual for the relatives to visit the grave, and to recite selections from the Qurán. Those who can afford to pay Maulavís, employ these learned men to recite the whole of the Qurán at the graves of their deceased relatives; and, as we have already remarked, in a former article, the Qurán is divided into sections to admit of its being recited by the several Maulavís at once. During the days of mourning the relatives abstain from wearing any article of dress of a bright colour, and their soiled garments remain unchanged.

References

1. The Shía'hs stand opposite the loins of a man.
2. This sentence is not generally recited in the Subhán of the daily prayer.
3. *Vide* article on Angles.

42
The Khutbah, or the Friday's Sermon

The *Khutbah* is the oration or sermon delivered in the mosque every Friday, and on the chief festivals,[1] after the meridian prayer. After the usual ablutions, the four *Sunnat* prayers are recited. The *Khatīb*, or preacher, then seats himself on the *Mimbar* (pulpit), whilst the Muazzin proclaims the Azán; after which he stands up on the second step,[2] and delivers the sermon, which must be in the Arabic language, and include prayers for "Muhammad, the Companions, and the King." There are several books of *Khutbahs* published for the use of preachers. The most celebrated of these preachers' manuals is the Mujmua' Khitáb, printed by Abdur Rahman of Cawnpore. The sermons are arranged for every Friday in the year, and are the compositions of various Muslim divines. It is remarkable that short sermons are meritorious; for it is related that the "Prophet" remarked that, "the length of a man's prayers and the shortness of his sermon are the signs of his sense and understanding; therefore, make your prayers long and your Khutbah short."

The following is a translation of the third Khutbah in the book of sermons already mentioned; it is a fair specimen of an average Khutbah, both as to its length and matter:—

"In the name of God, the compassionate, the merciful.

"Praised be God. Praised be that God who hath shown us the way in this religion. If He had not guided us into the path we should not have found it.

"I bear witness that there is no deity but God. He is one. He has no associate. I bear witness that Muhammad is, of a truth. His servant and His Apostle. May God have mercy upon him, and upon his descendants, and upon his companions, and give them peace.

"Fear God, O ye people, and fear that day, the day of judgment, when a father will not be able to answer for his son, nor the son for the father. Of a truth God's promises are true. Let not this present life make you proud. Let not the deceiver (Satan) lead you astray.

"O ye people who have believed, turn ye to God, as Nasuá[3] did turn to God. Verily God doth forgive all sin, verily He is the merciful, the forgiver of sins. Verily He is the most munificent, and bountiful, the King, the Holy One, the Clement, the Most Merciful."

The preacher then descends from the pulpit, and sitting on the floor of the mosque, offers up a silent prayer. He then, again, ascends the *Mimbar*, as before, and proceeds thus:—

"In the name of God, the compassionate, the merciful.

"Praised be God. We praise Him. We seek help from Him. We ask forgiveness of sins. We trust in Him. We seek refuge in Him from evil desires and from former sinful actions. He who has God for his guide is never lost; and whomsoever He leadeth aside none can guide into the right path.

"We bear witness that there is no deity but God. He is one. He hath no partner.

"Verily we bear witness that Muhammad is the servant and apostle of God, and may God have mercy upon him, who is more exalted than any being. May God have mercy upon his descendants, and upon his companions. May God give them peace! Especially upon Amír-ul-Mominín Abu Bakr Sadíq (may God be pleased with him). And upon him who was the most temperate of the "friends" Amír-ul-Mominín Omar Ibn-ul-Khattáb (may God be pleased with him). And upon him whose modesty and faith were perfect, Amír-ul-Mominín Osmán (may God be pleased with him). And upon the Lion of the powerful God, Amír-ul-Mominín Ali ibn Abu-Tálib (may God be pleased with him). And upon the two Imams, the holy ones, the two martyrs, Amír-ul-Mominín Abu Muhammad Hasan and Abu Abdullah Husain (may God be pleased with both of them). And upon the mother of these two persons, the chief of women, Fatimah-uz-Zárah (may God be pleased with her). And upon his (Muhammad's) two uncles, Hamza and 'Abbás (may God be pleased with them). And upon the rest of the "companions," and upon the "followers" (may God be pleased with all of them). Of Thy mercy, O most merciful of all merciful ones, O God, forgive all Musalmán men and Musalmán women, all male believers, and all female believers. Of a truth thou art He who wilt receive our prayers.

"O God, help those who help the religion of Muhammad. May we also exert ourselves to help those who help Islám. Make those weak, who weaken the religion of Muhammad.

"O God, bless the king of the age, and make him kind and favourable to the people.

"O servants of God, may God have mercy upon you. Verily, God enjoineth justice and the doing of good, and gifts to kindred; and He forbiddeth wickedness, and wrong, and oppression. He warneth you that haply ye may be mindful.[4]

"O ye people, remember the great and exalted God. He will also remember you. He will answer your prayers. The remembrance of God is great, and good, and honourable, and noble, and meritorious, and worthy, and sublime."

The preacher then descends, and taking up his position as Imám, facing the *Mihrab*,[5] conducts two *rak'at* prayers. The Khatíb, however, does not always officiate as Imám.

In Turkey and Egypt, and in other countries under Muslim rule, it is the custom for the Khatíb to deliver the Khutbah whilst he holds a wooden sword reversed.

The prayer for the reigning monarch, if he be a Muslim, would be offered up in the following manner:—

"O God, aid Islám, and strengthen its pillars, and make infidelity to tremble, and destroy its might, by the preservation of Thy servant, and the son of Thy servant, the submissive to the might of Thy Majesty and Glory, whom God hath aided, our master Amír Sher 'Alí Khán, son of Amír Dost Muhammad Khán, may God assist him and prolong his reign. O God, assist him, and assist his armies. O Thou God of the religion and Lord of the world, assist the armies of Muslims; frustrate the armies of infidels and polytheists, thine enemies, the enemies of the religion."

References

1. The 'Id-i-Fitr and the 'Id-ul-Azha.
2. The Mimbar is the pulpit of a mosque. It consists of three steps, and is sometimes a movable wooden structure, and sometimes a fixture of brick or stone built against the wall. Muhammad, in addressing the congregation, stood on the uppermost step, Abu Bakr on the second, and Omar on the third or the lowest. Osmán, being the most modest of the Khalifs, would have gladly descended lower if he could have done so; but this being impossible, he fixed upon the second step, from which it is still the custom to preach.

3. *Nasuá* is the name which occurs in the sixth verse of the Súrat-i-Tahrímah (lxvi.) in the Qurán; it is translated "true repentance by Sale and Rodwell, but it is supposed to be a person's name by several commentators.

4. The ninety-second verse of Súrat-i-Nahe (cxvi.) of the Qurán.

5. The Mihráb is the centre of the wall of a mosque, facing mecca, to which the Imám (priest) prays. It usually consists of a circular niche in the wall.

43
Jihád, or Religious War

Jihád[1] (lit. "an effort") is a religious war against the infidels, as enjoined by Muhammad in the following passages in the Qurán:—

Súrat-un-Nisà (vi.).

"Fight, therefore, for the religion of God."[1]

*   *   *   *   *   *   *

God hath indeed promised Paradise to every one,

But God hath preferred those who *fight for the faith.*"

Súrat-ul-Muhammad (xlvii.).

"Those who *fight in defence of God's true religion*,

God will not suffer their works to perish."

Those who engage in war against the infidels are called *Gházís*.

The Sunnís and Shía'hs alike believe in the eventual triumph of Islám, when the whole world shall become followers of the Prophet of Arabia; but whilst the Sunnís are, of course, ready to undertake the accomplishment of this great end, "whenever there is a probability of victory to the Musulmáns" the Shíá'hs, true to the one great principle of their sect, must wait until the appearance of a rightful Imám.

When an infidel's country is conquered by a Muslim

ruler, its inhabitants are offered three alternatives:—

1. *The reception of Islám*, in which case the conquered become enfranchised citizens of the Muslim state.
2. *The payment of a poll tax* (*Jizíyah*), by which unbelievers in Islám obtain protection, and become *Zimmi's.*
3. *Death by the sword.*

In a state brought under Muslims, all those who do not embrace the faith are placed under certain disabilities. They can worship God according to their own customs, *provided they are not idolators*; but it must be done without any ostentation, and, whilst churches and synagogues may be repaired, *no new place of worship can be erected. Vide* Hidáyah,[2] where we read:— "The construction of churches, or synagogues, in Muslim territory is unlawful, this being forbidden in the Traditions; but if places of worship belonging to Jews, or Christians, be destroyed, or fall into decay, they are at liberty to repair them, because buildings cannot endure for ever."

Idol temples must be destroyed, and idolatry suppressed by force in all countries ruled according to strict Muslim law.

References

1 Some Muhammadan divines say there are two Jiháds, *viz.*, Jihád-ul-Akbar, or the Greater Warfare, which is against one's own lusts; and Jihád-ul-Asghar, or the Lesser Warfare, against infidels.

2. Hamilton's Translation, vol. ii., p. 219.

44
Martyrs

The title of *Shahíd*, or martyr, is given to anyone who dies under the following circumstances:—

1. A soldier who dies in war for the cause of Islám.
2. One who innocently meets with his death from the hand of another.
3. The victim of a plague.
4. A person accidentally drowned.
5. One upon whom a wall may fall accidentally.
6. A person burnt in a house on fire.
7. One who dies from hunger.
8. One who dies on the pilgrimage to Mecca.

If a martyr dies in war, or is innocently murdered, he is buried without the usual washing before burial, as it is said that the blood of a martyr is a sufficient ablution.

45
The Four Orthodox Sects

There are four orthodox sects or schools of interpretation amongst the Sunnís, the Hanifi, the Sháfa'í, the Málikí, and the Hambalí.

1. The Hanifis are found in Turkey, Central Asia, and North India. The founder of this sect was Imám Abu Hanífa, who was born at Koofa, the capital of Irák, A.D. 702, or A.H. 80, at which time four of the "Prophet's" companions were still alive. He is the great oracle of jurisprudence, and (with his two pupils Imám Abu Yusaf and Imám Muhammad) was the founder of the Hanifi Code of Law[1].
2. The Sháfa'ías are found in South India and Egypt. The founder of this school of interpretation was Imám Muhammad ibn i Idrís al Shafa'í, who was born at Askalon, in Palestine, A.D. 772 (A.H. 150).
3. The Málikís prevail in Morocco, Barbary, and other parts of Africa, and were founded by Imám Málik, who was born at Madina, A.D. 717 (A.H. 93). He enjoyed the personal acquaintance of Hanífa, and he was considered the most learned man of his time.

4. The Hambalis were founded by Imám Abu 'Abdulláh ahmad ibn Muhammad ibn Hambal, who was born at Bagdad, A.D. 786 (A.H. 164). He attended the lectures delivered by Shafa'í, by whom he was instructed in the traditions. His followers are found in Eastern Arabia, and in some parts of Africa, but it is the least popular of the four schools of interpretation. They have no Muftí at Mecca, whilst the other three sects are represented there. The Wahhábís rose from this sect.

From the disciples of these four great Imáms have proceeded an immense number of commentaries and other works, all differing on a variety of points in their constructions, although coinciding in their general principles.

Reference

1. A Digest of the Hanifi Code of Law has been published in English by Mr. N.B.F. Baillie.

46
The Shía'hs

The Shía'hs (lit. "followers") are the followers of 'Ali, the husband of Fatimah, the daughter of Muhammad. They maintain that 'Ali was the first legitimate Khalífa, or successor to Muhammad, and therefore, reject Abu Bakr, Omar, and Osmán, the first three Khalifas, as usurpers. According to the Shía'hs the Muslim religion consists of a knowledge of the true *Imám*, or leader, and the differences amongst themselves with reference to this question have given rise to endless divisions. Of the proverbial seventy-three sects of Islám, not fewer than thirty-two are assigned to the Shía'hs.

The twelve Imáms, according to the Shía'hs, are as follows:—

1. Hazrat 'Ali.
2. Hasan.
3. Husain.
4. Zain-ul-'Abidín.
5. Muhammad Báqr.
6. Jáfir Sádiq.
7. Músa Kázim.
8. 'Ali Músa Razá.
9. Muhammad Taqí.

10. Muhammad Naqí.
11. Hasan 'Askarí.
12. Abu Qásim (or Imám Mahdí).

The last Imám, Abu Qásim, is supposed by the Shía'hs to be still alive and concealed in some secret place; and that he is the same Mahdí, or director, concerning whom Muhammad prophesied that the world should not have an end until one of his own descendants should govern the Arabians, and whose coming in the last days is expected by all Muslims.

During the absence of the Imám, the Shía'hs appeal to the *Mujtahids*, or enlightened doctors of the law, for direction in all matters both temporal and spiritual. Since the accession of Ismaíl, the first of the Sufí dynasty, A.D. 1499, the Shía'h faith has been the national religion of Persia. The enmity which exists between Sunní and Shía'h Muhammadans is, perhaps, hardly equalled by the mutual animosity which too often exists between Romanists and Protestants.

It is not true that the Shía'h Muhammadans reject the Traditions of Muhammad, although the Sunnís arrogate to themselves the title of traditionists. They do not acknowledge the *Siháh-i-Sita*, or six correct books of the Sunnís and Wahhábís, but receive the five collections of Traditions, entitled: 1. Káfi; 2. Man-lá-yastahzirah-al-Faqíh; 3. Tahzíb; 4. Istibsár; 5. Nahaj-ul-Balághat.

The Shía'h school of law is called the Imamía,[1] and it is earlier than that of the Sunnís; for Abu Hanífa, the father of the Sunní code of law, received his first instructions in jurisprudence from Imám Jáfir Sádiq, the sixth Imám of the Shía'hs; but this learned doctor afterwards separated from his teacher, and established a school of his own.

The differences between the Shía'hs and Sunnís are very numerous, but we will enumerate a few of them:—

1. The discussion as to the office of Imám, already alluded to.
2. The Shía'hs have a profound veneration for Imám 'Ali, and some of their sects regard him as an incarnation of divinity. They all assert that next to the Prophet, 'Ali is the most excellent of men.
3. They observe the ceremonies of the Muharram in commemoration of 'Ali, Hasan, Husain, and Bíbí Fatimah, whilst the Sunnís only regard the tenth day of Muharram, the *'Áshúráa*, being the day on which God is said to have created Adam and Eve, etc.
4. The Shía'hs permit Muta'h, or temporary marriages, which are contracted for a limited period, and for a certain sum of money. The Sunnís say that Muhammad afterwards cancelled this institutions.
5. The Shía'hs include the *Majusí*, or fire-worshippers, among the *Ahl-i-Kitáb*, or people of the Book, whilst Sunnís only acknowledge Jews, Christians, and Muslims, as *Kitábíahs.*
6. There are also various minor differences in the ceremony of *Sulát*, or prayer, and in the ablutions previous to prayer.
7. The Shía'hs admit a principle of religious compromise which is called *Takía* (lit. "guarding one's self"), a pious fraud whereby the Shía'h Muhammadan believes he is justified in either smoothing down or in denying the peculiarities of his religious belief in order to save himself from religious persecution. A Shía'h can,

therefore, pass himself off as a Sunní, or even curse the twelve Imáms, in order to avoid persecution.

Reference

1. A Digest of the Imámía code has been published by Mr. N. B. E. Baillie, London, 1869.

47
The Wahhábís

This sect was founded by Muhammad, son of Abdul Wahháb, but as their opponents could not call them *Muhammadans,* they have been distinguished by the name of the father of the founder of their sect, and are called Wahhábís.[1]

Shekh Muhammad was born at Ayína, a village in the province of Arad, in the country of Najd, in the year A.D. 1691. Having been carefully instructed in the tenets of the Muslim religion, according to the teachings of the Hambalí sect, he in due time left his native place, in company with his father, to perform the pilgrimage to Mecca. At Madina, he was instructed by Shekh Abdullah-ibn-Ibrahím, of Najd; and, it is supposed, that whilst sitting at the feet of this celebrated teacher, the son of Abdul Wahháb first realized how far the rigid lines of Islám had been stretched, almost to breaking, in the endeavour to adapt its stern principles to the superstitions of idolatrous Arabia. He accompanied his father to Harimala, and, after his father's death, he returned to his native village of Ayína, where he assumed the position of a religious teacher. His teachings met with acceptance, and he soon acquired so great an influence over the people of those parts that the Governor of Hassa compelled him to leave the district, and the reformer found a friendly asylum in

Deraiah, under the protection of Muhammad-ibn-Saud, a chief of considerable influence, who made the protection of Ibn-Abdul-Wahháb a pretext for a war with the Shekh of Hassa. Ibn Saud married the daughter of Ibn-Abdul-Wahháb, and established in his family the Wahhábí dynasty, which, after a chequered existence of more than a hundred years, still exists in the person of the Wahhábí chief at Ryadh.[2]

The whole of Eastern Arabia has embraced the reformed doctrines of the Wahhábís, and Mr. Palgrave, in his account of his travels in those parts, has given an interesting sketch of the Wahhábí religionists, although he is not always correct as to the distinctive principles of their religious creed.

In the great Wahhábí revival, political interests were united with religious reform, as was the case in the great Puritan struggle in England; and the Wahhábís soon pushed their conquests over the whole of Arabia. In A.D. 1803, they conquered Mecca and Madina, and for many years threatened the subjugation of the whole Turkish Empire; but in A.D. 1811, Muhammad 'Ali, the celebrated Pasha of Egypt, commenced a war against the Wahhábís, and soon recovered Mecca and Madina; and in 1818, his son, Ibrahím Pasha, totally defeated Abdullah, the Wahhábí leader, and sent him a prisoner to Constantinople, where he was executed in the public square of St. Sophia, December 19th, 1818. But although the temporal power of the Wahhábís has been subdued, they still continue secretly to propagate their peculiar tenets, and in the present day there are numerous disciples of the sect not only in Arabia, but in Turkey and in India. It is a movement which has influenced religious thought in every part of Islám.

The Wahhábís speak of themselves as *Muwahhid,* or Unitarians, and call all others *Mushrik*, or those who associate another with God; and the following are some of their distinctive religious tenets:—

1. They do not receive the decisions of the four orthodox sects, but say that any man who can read and understand the Qurán and the sacred Hadís can judge for himself in matters of doctrine. They, therefore, reject *Ijma'* after the death of the Companions of the Prophet.
2. That no one but God can know the secrets of men, and that prayers should not be offered to any Prophet, Walí, Pír, or Saint; but that God may be asked to grant a petition for the *sake* of a saint.
3. That at the last day, Muhammad will obtain permission (*izn*) of God to intercede for his people. The Sunnís believe that permission has already been given.
4. That it is unlawful to illuminate the shrines of departed saints, or to prostrate before them, or to perambulate (*tawáf*) round them.
5. That women should not be allowed to visit the graves of the dead, on account of their immoderate weeping.
6. That only four festivals ought to be observed, namely, 'Id-ul-Fitr, 'Id-ul-Azhá, 'Áshúráa, and Shab-i-Barát.
7. They do not observe the ceremonies of *Maulúd*, which are celebrated on the anniversary of Muhammad's birth.
8. They do not present offerings (*Nazr*) at any shrine.

9. They count the ninety-nine names of God on their fingers, and not on a rosary.
10. They understand the terms "sitting of God," and "hand of God," which occur in the Qurán, in their literal (*Haqíqí*) sense, and not figuratively (*Majázi*); but, at the same time, they say it is not revealed *how* God sits, or in what sense he has a hand, etc.[4]

References

1. *Vide* a Wahhábí book entitled Sulh-ul-Aklwán, by Sayyid Allama Daud, of Bagdad.
2. The following are the names of the Wahhabí chiefs, from the establishment of the dynasty: — Muhammad-ibn-Saud, died A.D. 1765; Abdul-Azíz, assassinated 1803; Saud-ibn-Abdul Azíz, died 1814; Abdullah-ibn-Saud, beheaded 1818; Turkí, assassinated 1830; Fayzul, died 1866; Abdullah, still living. Fayzul and his son Abdullah entertained Col. Sir Lewis Pelly, K.C.B., K.C.S.I., who visited the Wahhábí capital as Her Britannic Majesty's representative, in 1865.
3. The remnant of the Sayyid's army formed the nucleus of the Wahhábí fanatics, who are now stationed at the village of Polosí, on the banks of the Indus, on the north-west frontier of British India.
4. On this account the Christian doctrines of the Trinity and the Sonship of Christ do not present the same difficulties to the mind of a Wahhábi which they do to that of a Sunní.

48
Sufi'ism or Mysticism

The term *Súfi´* is said to be derived from the Arabic *Súf*, "wool," on account of the woollen garments worn by the Eastern ascetics; or from the Persian *Sáf*, "pure," with reference to the Sufiístic effort to attain to metaphysical purity; or from the Greek, *σvøια*, "wisdom," *i.e.*, the true wisdom, or knowledge.

Tasawwaf, or Sufiísm, appears to be but the Muslim adaptation of the doctrines of the Vedanta school, which we also find in the writings of the old academies of Greece, and which Sir William Jones thought Plato learned from the sages of the East.

The Súfis are divided into innumerable sects; but although they differ in name and in some of their customs, they are all agreed in the principal tenets, especially those which inculcate the absolute necessity of blind submission to an inspired teacher, or *Murshid.* They believe that God only exists. He is in all things, and all things in him, and all created beings visible and invisible are an emanation from God, and not really distinct from Him. That the soul of man existed before the body in which it is confined as in a cage. The great object of the Súfí being to escape from the trammels of humanity, and to return to the bosom of divinity, whilst the teachings of their mystic creed are supposed to lead the soul onward, stage by stage, until it reaches the goal—*perfect knowledge.*

The natural state of every Muslim is *Násút*, in which state the disciple must observe the precepts of the law, or *Shari'at*; but, as this is the lowest form of spiritual existence, the performance of the *journey* is enjoined upon every searcher after Truth.

The following are the stages (*Manzil*) which the Súfí has to perform. Having become a searcher after God (*Tálib*), he enters the first stage of *'Ubúdíyat*, "service". When the Divine attraction has developed his inclination into the love of God, he is said to have reached the second stage of *'Ishaq*, "love". This Divine love, expelling all worldly desires from his heart, he arrives at the third stage of *Zudh*, "seclusion". Occupying himself henceforward with contemplation and the investigations of the metaphysical theories concerning the nature, attributes, and works of God, which are the characteristics of the Sífí system, he reaches the fourth stage of *M'arijat*, "knowledge". This assiduous contemplation of metaphysical theories soon produces a state of mental excitement, which is considered a sure prognostication of direct illumination from God. This fifth stage is called *Wajd*, "ecstasy". During the next stage he is supposed to receive a revelation of the true nature of the Godhead, and to have reached the sixth stage of *Haqíqat*, "truth". The next stage is that of *Wasl*, "union with God," which is the highest stage to which he can go whilst in the body; but when death overtakes him, it is looked upon as a total re-absorption into the Deity, forming the consummation of his journey and the eighth and last stage of *Faná*, "extinction". That stage in which the traveller is said to have attained to the love of God, is the point from which the Sufiístic poets love to discuss the doctrines of their sect. The *Sálik*, or traveller, is the Lover (*'Áshiq*), and God is the Beloved One (*M'ashuq*). This Divine love is the theme of most of the Persian and Pushtu poems, which abound in Sufiístic expressions which are difficult of interpretation to an ordinary English reader. For instance, *Sharáb,* "wine," expresses the domination of Divine love in the heart. *Gísú*, "a ringlet," the details of the mysteries of Divinity. *Mai Khána*, "a tavern," a stage of the journey. "Mirth," "wantonness," and "inebriation," signify religious enthusiasm and abstraction from worldly things.

The eight stages which we have given are those usually taught by Súfí teachers in their published works; but in North India we have frequently met with persons of this sect, who have learnt only the four following stages:—

"The first, *Násút*, 'humanity," for which there is the *Sharí'at*, or law. The second, *Malakút*, "the nature of angles," for which there is *Taríqât,* or the pathway of purity. The third is *Jabarút*, "the possession of power," for which there is *M'arifat*, or knowledge. And the fourth is *Láhút*, "extinction," for which there is *Haqíqat*, or truth.

The Súfí mystic seeks, by concentration of his thoughts and affections on God, to lose his own identity; and the following fable, related by Jalál-ud-dín, the author of the Masnawí,[1] illustrates their views on the subject. It represents Human Love seeking admission into the Sanctuary of Divinity:—

"One knocked at the door of the Beloved, and a voice from within inquired 'Who is there?' Then he answered, '*It is I.*' And the voice said, 'This house will not hold me and thee. So the door remained shut. Then the Lover sped away into the wilderness, and fasted and prayed in solitude. And after a year he returned, and knocked again at the door, and the voice again demanded, 'Who is there?' And the Lover said, '*It is Thou.*' Then the door was opened."

In Professor Max Müller's address to the Aryan section of the International Congress of Orientalists assembled in London, in September, 1874, he said:—"We have learnt already one lesson, that behind the helpless expressions which language was devised, whether in the East or the West, for uttering the unutterable * * * there is the same intention, the same striving, the same stammering, the same faith. Other lessons will follow, till in the end we shall be able to restore that ancient word which unites not only the East with the West, but with all the members of the human family, and may learn to understand what a Persian poet meant when he wrote many centuries ago:—'Diversity of worship has divided the human race into seventy-two nations. From all their dogmas I have selected one—the love of God.' "

References

1. The Masnawí is the celebrated book of the Súfí mystics which, it is said, takes the place of the Qurán amongst the majority of people in Persia.

49
Faqírs, or Darweshes

The Arabic word *Faqír*, signifies poor; but it is used in the sense of being in need of mercy, and poor in the sight of God, rather than in need of worldly assistance. *Darwesh* is derived from the Persian *dar*, "a door," —those who beg from door to door. The terms are generally used for those who lead a religious life. Religious Faqírs are divided into two great classes, the *ba Sahra'* (with the law), or those who govern their conduct according to the principles of Islám; and the *be Shara'* (without the law) or those who do not rule their lives according to the principles of any religious creed, although they call themselves Musulmáns. The former are called *Sálik*, or travellers on the pathway (*taríquat*) to heaven; and the latter are either *Ázád* (free), or *Majzúb* (abstracted). The *Sálik* embrace the various religious orders who perform the Zikrs described in our next note. The *Majzúb* are totally absorbed in religious reverie. The *Ázád* shave their beards, whiskers, moustachios, eyebrows and eyelashes, and lead lives of celibacy.

The *Ázád* and *Majzúb* Faqírs can scarcely be said to be Muhammadans, so that a description of their various sects do not fall within the limits of these notes. The Sálik Faqírs are also divided into very numerous orders, but their chief difference consists in their *Silsilah*, or chain of succession, from their great teachers the Khalífas 'Ali, and

Abu Bakr, who are said to have been the founders of the religious order of Faqírs. Europeans writers have distinguished the various orders by their dress and their religious performances; but we have not been able to find that these are the distinguishing features of difference amongst them :

The following are the chief orders which are met with in North India :—

1. The Naqshbandía are followers of Khwájah Pír Muhammad Naqshband, and are a very numerous sect; they usually perform the *Zikr-i-Khafí*, or the silent religious devotion described in the next chapter.
2. The Qádiría sprung from the celebrated Sayyid Abdul Qádir, surnamed Pír Dustagír, whose shrine is at Bagdad. They practise both the *Zikr-i-Jalí*, and the *Zikr-i-Khafí*. Most of the Sunní Maulavís on the north-west frontier of India are members of this order. In Egypt it is most popular amongst fishermen.
3. The Chishtía are followers of Banda Nawáz, surnamed the *Gaysu daráz*, or the long-ringletted. His shrine is at Calburgah.

   The Shía'hs generally become Faqírs of this order. They are partial to vocal music, for the founder of the order remarked, that singing was the food and support of the soul. They perform the *Zikr-i-Jalí*, described in the next article.
4. The Jalália were founded by Sayyid Jalál-ud-dín, of Bokhára. They are met with in Central Asia. Religious mendicants are often of this order.
5. The Sarwardía are a popular order in Afghanistan, and comprise a number of learned men. They are the followers of Hasan Bisrí, of Basra, near Bagdad.

No.	*Name of the Order*	*Founder*	*Place of the Founder's Shrine*	*Date A.H.*
1.	Alwáni	Shekh Alwán	Jeddah	149
2.	Adhamí	Ibrahim ibn Adham	Damascus	161
3.	Bastámí	Bayazid Bastámí	Jebel Bestámí	261
4.	Saqatí	Sirrí Siqatí	Bagdad	295
5.	Qádirí	Abdul-Qádir Jiláni	Bagdad	561
6.	Rufálí	Syyid Ahmad Rufáh	Bagdad	576
7.	Sahrwardi	Shiháb-ud-din	Bagdad	602
8.	Kabrawí	Najm-ud-dín	Khwaresm	617
9.	Shádilí	Abul Hasan	Mecca	656
10.	Maulaví	Jalál-ud-dín Mulána	Conyah	672
11.	Badawí	Abul Fitan Ahmad	Egypt	675
12.	Naqshbandí	Pir Muhammad	Persia	719
13.	S'adí	S'ad-ud-dín	Damascus	736
14.	Bakhtáshi	Haji Bakhtásh	Kir Sher	736
15.	Khilwatí	'Umar Khilwatí	Caisarea	800
16.	Zainí	Zain-ud-dín	Cufa	838
17.	Bahái	Abdul Ghani	Adrianople	870
18.	Bairamí	Haji Bairam	Angora	876
19.	Ashrafí	Ashraf Rumi	Chín Iznic	899
20.	Bakrí	Abu Bakr Wafái	Aleppo	902
21.	Sunbuli	Sunbul Yusuf Bolawí	Constantinople	936
22.	Ghulshaní	Ibrahím Ghulshaní	Cairo	940
23.	Yíjit Báshí	Shams-ud-dín	Magnesia	951
24.	Umm Sunání	Shekh Umm Sunán	Constantinople	959
25.	Jalwatí	Pir Uftadí	Bursah	958
26.	'Usháqi	Hasan-ud-din	Constantinople	1001
27.	Shamsí	Shams-ud-dín	Madina	1010
28.	Sinan Umamí	'Alim Sinam Ummí	Elmahlí	1079
29.	Niyázi	Muhammad Niyáz	Lemnos	1100
30.	Mas'adí	Murád Shámí	Constantinople	1132
31.	Nuruddiní	Nur-ud-dín	Constantinople	1146
32.	Jamálí	Jamál-ud-dín	Constantinople	1164

These are the most noted orders of *ba Shara'* Faqírs. The *be Shara'* Faqírs are very numerous. The most popular order is that of the *Mudáría*, founded by Zinda Sháh Murdár, of Syria, whose shrine is at Mukanpur, in Oudh. From these have sprung the *Malang* Faqírs who crowd the bazaars of India. They wear their hair matted, and tied in a knot. The Rafia order is also a numerous one in some parts of India. They practise the most severe discipline, and mortify themselves by beating their bodies.

D'Ohsson enumerates thirty-two of the principal religious orders, giving the name of the founder, and the place of his shrine.

We insert the above list on the authority of M. D'Ohsson; but we have not had an opportunity of testing the correctness of its information.

The order of Maulavís is the most popular religious order in Constantinople. They are called by Europeans the dancing, or whirling darweshes, and their religious performances constitute one of the public sights in Constantinople. They have service at their *Takiya*, or convent, every Wednesday, and at Kasim Pasha every Sunday, at 2 o'clock. There are about twenty performers, with high round felt caps and brown mantles. At a given signal they all fall flat on their faces, and rise and walk slowly round and round with their arms folded, bowing and turning slowly several times. They then cast off their mantles and appear in long bell-shaped petticoats and jackets, and then begin to spin, revolving, dancing, and turning with extraordinary velocity.

The founder of this religious order was a native of Balkh, in Central Asia. It is said the spiritual powers of this extraordinary man were developed at the early age of six years; for once on a Friday Jalál-ud-dín was at Balkh on the roof of a house with some children of his own age, when one of the boys asked him if it were possible for him to jump from one house to the other. He replied, "If you have faith, jump up towards heaven." He then sprang upwards and was immediately lost to sight. The youths all cried out as he disappeared, but he soon returned from the celestial regions, greatly altered in complexion and changed in figure; for he had obtained a sight of the abodes of bliss.

It is impossible to become acquainted with all the rules and ceremonies of the numerous orders of Faqírs; for, like those of the Free-masons, they may not be divulged to the uninitiated.

The following is said to be the usual method of admitting a Muhammadan to the order of a *ba Shara'* Faqír. Having first performed the legal ablutions, the *Muríd* (disciple) seats himself before the *Murshid* (spiritual guide). The Murshid then takes the Murid's right hand, and requires of him a confession of sin according to the following form: "I ask forgiveness of the great God than Whom there is no other deity, the Eternal, the Everlasting, the Living One: I turn to Him for repentance, and beg His grace and forgiveness." This, or a similar form of repentance, is repeated several times. The Muríd then repeats after the Murshid: "I beg for the favour of God and of the Prophet, and I take for my guide to God (here naming the Murshid) not to change or to separate. God is our witness. By the great God. There is no deity but God. Amín." The Murshid and the Muríd then recite the first chapter of the Qurán, and the Muríd concludes the ceremony by kissing the Murshid's hand.

After the initiatory rite, the Muríd undergoes a series of instructions, including the *Zikrs*, which he is required to repeat daily. The Muríd frequently visits his Murshid, and sometimes the Murshids proceed on a circuit of visitation to their disciples. The place where these "holy men" sit down to instruct the people is ever afterwards held sacred, a small flag is hoisted on a tree, and it is fenced in. Such places are called "*Takiya*," and are protected and kept free from pollution by some Faqír engaged for the purpose.

Those Faqírs who attain to a high degree of sanctity are called *Walís*, the highest rank of which is that of a *Ghaus*. Of such is the Akhund of Swát, on the north-west frontier of India. This celebrated religious leader at the age of eighteen became a member of the Qádiría order of Faqírs; and shortly after his incorporation, he settled down on a small island in the river Indus near Attock, where he lived the life of a recluse for twelve years. During this time, it is said, his only diet was the wild-grass seed and buffalo's milk. He soon acquired a reputation for sanctity, and has gradually become the great religious leader of Central Asia. He now resides at the village of Seydu in Swát, where he entertains as many as a thousand visitors daily; men from all parts of the Muslim world, who come to bear his wisdom and receive the benefit of his prayers. The Akhund has always been a great opponent of Wahhábí doctrines; and, although he is not well-read in Muslim divinity, his *fatwás* on religious ceremonies and secular observances are received and obeyed by all the Sunní Muhammadans of the north-west frontier of British India.[1]

Reference

1. An account of the Muhammadan darweshes has been written by Mr. J.P. Brown, Secretary of the United States Legation at Constantinople. Trüh & Co., London.

50
Zikr, or the Religious Services of the Darweshes

Zikr is the religious ceremony, or act of devotion, which is practised by the various religious orders of Faqírs, or Darweshes. Almost every religious Muhammadan is a member of some order of Faqírs, and, consequently, the performance of *zikr* is very common in all Muhammadan countries; but it does not appear that anyone method of performing the religious service of *zikr*, is peculiar to any particular order.

Zikrs, are of two kinds, *zikr-i-jalí*, that which is recited aloud, and *zikr-i-khafí*, that which is performed either with a low voice, or mentally.

The Naqshbandía order of Faqírs usually perform the latter, whilst the Chishtía and Qádiría orders celebrate the former. There are various ways of going through the exercise, but the main features of each are similar in character. The following is a *zikr-i-jali* as given in the book Qual-ul-Jamíl, by Maulaví Sháh Walí Ullah, of Delhi:—

1. The worshipper sits in the usual sitting posture and shouts the word *Al-lah* (God), drawing his voice from his left side and then from his throat.
2. Sitting as at prayers he repeats the word *Al-lah* still louder than before, first from his right knee, and then from his left side.

3. Folding his legs under him he repeats the word *Al-lah* first from his right knee and then from his left side, still louder!

4. Still remaining in the same position, he shouts the word *Al-lah*, first from the left knee, then from the right knee, then from the left side, and lastly in front, still louder!

5. Sitting as at prayer, with his face towards Mecca, he closes his eyes, says "*Lá*"—drawing the sound as from his navel up to his left shoulder; then he says *i-lá-ha*, drawing out the sound as from his brain; and lastly, "*il-lal-lá-ho,*" repeated from his left side with great energy.

Each of these stages is called a *Zarb*. They are, of course, recited many hundreds of times over, and the changes we have described account for the variations of sound and motion of the body described by Eastern travellers who have witnessed the performance of a *zikr*.

The following is a *zikr-i-khafi*, or that which is performed in either a low voice, or mentally.

1. Closing his eyes and lips, he says, "with the tongue of the heart,"

   Al-la-ho-sami'un, "God the hearer."

   Al-la-ho-baswírun, "God the seer."

   Al-la-ho-'alimun, "God the knower."

   The first being drawn, as it were, from the navel to the breast; the second, from the breast to the brain; the third, from the brain up to the heavens; and then again repeated stage by stage backwards and forwards.

2. He says in a low voice, "*Allah*," from the right knee, and then from the left side.

3. With each exhalation of his breath, he says, "*lá-iláha,*" and with each inhalation, "*il-lal-lá-ho.*"

This third *zarb* is a most exhausting act of devotion, performed, as it is, hundreds or even thousands of times, and is, therefore, considered the most meritorious.

It is related that Maulaví Habíb Ullah, now living in the village of Gabásanri, in the Gadún country, on the Peshawur frontier, has become such an adept in the performance of this *zarb*, that he recites the first part of the *zikr-lá-iláha* with the exhalation of his breath after the mid-day prayer; and the second part, *il-lal-lá-ho,* with the inhalation of his breath before the next time of prayer, thus sustaining his breath for the period of about three hours!

Another act of devotion, which usually accompanies the *zikr*, is that of *Muráqaba*, or meditation.

The worshipper first performs *zikr* of the following:—

Allaho-házarí, "God the present one."

Allaho-názarí, "God the seer."

Allaho-sháhidí, "God who witnesses."

Allaho-maí, "God who is with us."

Having recited this *zikr*, either aloud or mentally, the worshipper proceeds to meditate upon some verse or verses of the Qurán. Those recommended for the Qádiría Faqírs by Maulavi Sháb Walí Ullah are the following, which we give as indicating the line of thought which is considered most devotional and spiritual by Muslim mystics:—

1. Surat-ul-Hadíd (lvii.), 3.

"He (God) is first. He is last. The Manifest, and the Hidden, and who knoweth all things."

2. Surat-ul-Hadíd (lvii.), 4.

"He (God) is with you wheresoever ye be."

3. Surat-ul-Qáf (1.), 16.

"We (God) are closer to him (man) than his neck vein."

4. Surat-ul-Baqr (ii.), 109.

"Whichever way ye turn, there is the face of God."

5. Surat-un-Nisá (iv.), 125.

"God encompasseth all things."

6. Surat-ur-Rahman (lv.), 7.

"All on earth shall pass away, but the face of thy God shall abide resplendent with majesty and glory."

Some teachers tell their disciples that the heart has two doors, that which is fleshy, and that which is spiritual; and that the *zikr-i-jalí* has been established for the opening of the former, and *zikr-i-khafí* for the latter, in order that they may both be enlightened.

There certainly must be something invigorating in the exercise of a *zikr-i-jalí* to a religious devotee, who seldom stirs out of his mosque; and we have often been told by Maulavís, that they find the performance of a *zikr* keeps evil thoughts from the mind; but as some of the most devoted *zákirs* (*i.e.,* those who perform the *zikr*) are amongst the most immoral men, the religious exercise does not appear to have any lasting effect on the moral character.

As a curious instance of the superstitious character of this devotional exercise, the Chishtía order believe that if a man sits cross-legged and seizes the vein called *Kaimás*, which is under the leg, with his toes, that it will give peace to his heart, when accompanied by a *zikr* of the "*nafí isbát*," which is a term used for the first part of the Kalimah, which forms the usual *zikr,* namely:—

Lá-ilázha-il-lal-laho, "There is no deity but God."

The most common form of *zikr* is a recital of the ninety-nine names of God; for Muhammad promised those of his followers who recited them, a sure entrance to Paradise.[1]

There are several lists of the supposed ninety-nine names[2] of God; but the following is given by Muslim and Bokhárí in their collections of traditions:—

1.	Rahmán	The Compassionate.
2.	Rahím	The Merciful.
3.	Málik	The King.
4.	Quddus	The Holy One.
5.	Salám	The Peace.
6.	Momin	The Faithful.
7.	Mohymin	The Protector.
8.	'Azíz	The Incomparable.
9.	Jabbár	The Benefactor.
10.	Mutakabbir	The Mighty Doer.
11.	Kháliq	The Creator.
12.	Bárí	The Maker.
13.	Musawwir	The Former
14.	Ghafár	The Pardoner.
15.	Qahhár.	The Powerful.
16.	Wahháb	The Giver.
17.	Razzáq	The Bestower of Daily Bread.
18.	Fattah	The Opener.
19.	'Alím	The Omniscient.
20.	Qábiz	The Restrainer.
21.	Básit	The Expander.
22.	Kháfiz	The Depresser
23.	Ráfí	The Exalter.

24.	Mu'iz	The Strengthener.
25.	Muzil	The Lowerer.
26.	Sami'	The Hearer.
27.	Basír	The Seer.
28.	Hákam	The Judge.
29.	'Adl	The Just.
30.	Latíf	The Benignant.
31.	Khabír	The Knower.
32.	Halím	The Clement.
33.	'Azím	The Great.
34.	Ghafúr	The Great Pardoner.
35.	Shakúr	The Rewarder.
36.	'Alí	The Most High.
37.	Kabír	The Great Lord.
38.	Háfiz	The Guardian.
39.	Muqít	The Giver of Strength.
40.	Hasíb	The Reckoner.
41.	Jalíl	The Glorious.
42.	Karím	The Munificent.
43.	Raqib	The Watcher
44.	Mujíb	The Approver of Supplications.
45.	Wási'	The Expander.
46.	Hakím	The Physician.
47.	Wadúd	The All-Loving.
48.	Majíd	The Glorious.
49.	Báis	The Awakener.
50.	Shahíd	The Witness.
51.	Haqq	The True.

52.	Wakíl	The Provider.
53.	Qawwí	The Powerful.
54.	Matín	The Firm.
55.	Walí	The Friend.
56.	Hamíd	The One to be Praised.
57.	Muhsí	The Counter.
58.	Mubdí	The Cause.
59.	Mu'íd	The Restorer.
60.	Mohyí	The Life-Giver.
61.	Mumit	The Death-Giver.
62.	Hai	The Living.
63.	Qaiyyúm	The Self-subsisting.
64.	Wájid	The Finder.
65.	Majíd	The Grand.
66.	Wáhid	The Unique.
67.	Samad	The Perpetual.
68.	Qádir	The Powerful.
69.	Muqtadir	The Prevailing.
70.	Muqaddim	The Bringer before.
71.	Muwakhkhir	The Bringer after.
72.	Awwal	The First.
73.	Akhir	The Last.
74.	Zahir	The Evident.
75.	Bátin	The Hidden.
76.	Wálí	The Governor.
77.	Muta'á	The Sublime.
78.	Barr	The Doer of Good.
79.	Tawwáb	The Propitious.

80.	Muntaqim	The Avenger.
81.	Afú	The Eraser.
82.	Ráuf	The Benefiter.
83.	Málik-ul-Mulk	The King of Kingdoms.
84.	Zuljalál-wal-Ikrám	The Lord of Glory and Honour.
85.	Muksit	The Equitable.
86.	Jámi'	The Assembler.
87.	Ghaní	The Rich.
88.	Mughaní	The Enricher.
89.	Mutí	The Giver.
90.	Maní'	The Withholder.
91.	Zárr	The Afflicter.
92.	Náfi	The Benefactor.
93.	Núr	The Light.
94.	Hádí	The Guide.
95.	Badia'	The Incomparable.
96.	Báqí	The Eternal.
97.	Wáris	The Inheritor.
98.	Rashíd	The Director.
99.	Sabúr	The Patient.

The list either begins or closes with the peculiar designation of God, *Allah*, making the complete number of one hundred names for the Deity.

The following names occur in other works which we have consulted, and are sometimes used in the place of some of those in the list already given:—*Azalí*, the Eternal; *Abadí*, the Everlasting; *Maula*, the Lord; *Ahad*, the only One; *Mun'em*, the Giver of Blessing; *Sádiq*, the Righteous One; *Sattár*, the Concealer of Sins, *Rabb*, the Lord.

In the recital of these words the prefix and inflexion are used thus, Ar-Rahímo ! Al-Máliko! As-Sami'o !, etc. Many of the titles will appear to the English reader to be synonymous, but Muslim theologians discover in them shades of difference. It will be observed that the titles are not arranged in philosophical order.

In addition to the forms of *zikr* already mentioned there are four others which are even of more common use, and are known as *Tasbíh, Tahmíd, Tahlíl*, and *Takbír*. They are used as exclamations of joy and surprise, as well as for the devotional exercise of *zikr.*

Tasbíh is the expression *Subhán-Allah!* "Holiness be to God !"

Tahmíd. Alhamdo-Lilla ! "Praise be to God !"

Tahlíl. Lá-il-la-ha-il-lal-lá-ho ! "There is no deity but God !"

Takbír. Allaho-Akbar ! "God is great !"

Muhammad said, "Repeat the Tasbíh a hundred times, and a thousand virtues shall be recorded by God for you, ten virtuous deeds for each repetition."

When the *Tasbíh* and *Tahmíd* are recited together it is said thus, *Subhán-ALlah wa Bihamdihi, i.e.*, "Holiness be to God with His praise." It is related in the Hadís that Muhammad said, "Whoever recites this sentence a hundred times, morning and evening, will have all his sins forgiven."

References

1. *Vide* Mishkát, bk. cxi.
2. Surat-al-Aráf (vii.), 179: "Most excellent titles hath God by these, call ye upon him."

Index